INDIANAPOLIS
Through Our Eyes

THE INDIANAPOLIS STAR
INDYSTAR★.COM | SEE WHAT HAPPENS

Copyright© 2003   •   ISBN: 1-932129-37-5

All rights reserved. No part of this book may be reproduced, stored in a retrieval system or transmitted in any form or by any means, electronic, mechanical, photocopying, recording or otherwise, without prior written permission of the copyright owner or the publisher.
Published by Pediment Publishing, a division of The Pediment Group, Inc.   www.pediment.com   printed in Canada

CONTENTS

A CITY OF PROMISE *1900-1909* 7

GROWTH & TRAGEDY *1910-1919* 15

ERA OF CHANGE, SHAME *1920-1929* 29

SURVIVING THE DEPRESSION *1930-1939* 37

UNITED WE STOOD *1940-1949* 47

THE GOOD LIFE *1950-1959* 61

TUMULTUOUS TIMES *1960-1969* 73

TURNING POINT *1970-1979* 93

A CITY TRANSFORMED *1980-1989* 101

A NEW MILLENNIUM *1990-2003* 113

ACKNOWLEDGMENTS

The Indianapolis Star wishes to thank the many people who made this book possible: the photographers, reporters, editors and newsmakers who have filled the pages of The Indianapolis Star for 100 years. Without them, this book, celebrating The Star's first 100 years, could not have been published.

Special credit for the development of this book goes to the following people and organizations:

Co-authors: Star Reporter Rob Schneider and Star Library Director Michael Jesse

Editor: Star Library Director Michael Jesse

Research and photo selection: Star Reference Librarian Dawn Mitchell

Photography advisor: Star Photographer Charlie Nye

Other contributors: Star Reference Librarian Barbara Hoffman and Star Features Copy Desk Chief Jim Lindgren

Special thanks to: The Indiana Historical Society Library staff

Project manager: Star Marketing Communications Manager Jennifer Gombach

FOREWORD

The Indianapolis Star celebrates its 100th birthday in June 2003. For those 10 decades, The Star has published words, pictures, ideas and opinions that reflect life in Indiana. Our photographers, reporters, editors, sales executives, press operators and delivery teams work diligently every day to provide our readers with the news and information that affects and reflects Hoosiers' lives.

While this book captures just a small portion of the past 100 years, we hope it provides a memorable journey through the history of our community, state and world. We have provided historic pictures – and historic front pages of The Star – to reflect not only major events, but also everyday moments in the life of our city, state and country.

The Star's future is inextricably tied to the future of the community we serve, and we proudly celebrate our first 100 years of service to the Central Indiana community. We promise to be here for you for the next 100 years – continuing the tradition of being Indiana's No. 1 provider of news and information.

Barbara A. Henry
President and Publisher

A CITY OF PROMISE
1900 - 1909

When The Indianapolis Star began publishing in 1903, it became part of a bustling city whose population had expanded by almost 10 times in the past 40 years. Railroads had produced the boom and by the turn of the century Indianapolis was flush with the belief that the city's time was at hand.

Just a year before The Star's launch, in 1902, the Soldiers and Sailors Monument was dedicated, honoring Civil War veterans. Tens of thousands of people had poured into the city for the dedication of the monument, which had taken nearly $600,000 and 14 years to build. The master of ceremonies for the day was Lew Wallace, whose book, *Ben-Hur*, had become a best seller. James Whitcomb Riley read a poem he had written for the occasion.

In addition to Riley, Indianapolis could claim several other literary stars of the day, including novelist Booth Tarkington.

In politics, the city had already produced a president, Benjamin Harrison, and in 1904 another Indianapolis resident, Charles W. Fairbanks, was elected to the vice-presidency under Theodore Roosevelt.

The city had also been the birthplace of a new political party when, in 1901, the Socialist Party of America was founded. One of the key players in the Socialist movement was Eugene V. Debs, of Terre Haute.

Photographs of downtown Indianapolis in the early 1900s show sidewalks jammed with people from building to curb, and streets a jumble of horse-drawn carriages and wagons, men on bicycles and streetcars.

Each day hundreds of passengers poured into the city center from 200 trains arriving at Union Station. The wholesale district, just south of Washington Street, was a place where everything imaginable, from household goods to tobacco and candy, could be found. Wagons rushed between Union Station and the wholesale businesses, delivering goods that formed mountains of crates along street fronts.

In 1903, the 450-room Claypool Hotel opened, with rooms furnished with mahogany dressers and brass beds. At the hotel owner's insistence, each room had a private bath. For many years it would be the city's finest hotel.

Two years later, in 1905, the city's first modern department store, L.S. Ayres & Co., went up on the southwest corner at Meridian and Washington streets. Meanwhile, the Wm. H. Block Co., which started out as a small store on East Washington, had its eye on the southwest corner of Illinois and Market streets for a new building, which would open in 1911.

As significant as the Soldiers and Sailors Monument was to Indianapolis' long-term identity, another symbol of the city's future was being created in a farm field west of the city. It was a test track for the emerging automobile industry and it would become known as the Indianapolis Motor Speedway.

The track was the brainchild of Carl Fisher, a poor boy from Greensburg who dropped out of school to go to work at age 12 and who moved to Indianapolis as a teen and joined his brothers in operating a bicycle shop at 112 N. Pennsylvania St. Bicycles weren't fast enough for Fisher, and he was soon racing cars. He opened an automobile showroom on North Illinois Street about 1902 and by the end of 1908 he formed a new venture with James Allison and others to build a race track for testing automobiles.

Automobiles were no longer just a curiosity, but a fortune-making venture, and as the speeds of cars went up, auto manufacturing companies were running out of places to test them. Fisher and Allison weren't planning to create a sporting event, but a place to demonstrate a car's proficiency.

The partners borrowed $250,000 to build the track and tried to recoup some of their investment through such public events as balloon, motorcycle and automobile races. But the events organized in 1909 were failures, and the original track broke apart under the pounding of speeding cars. Fisher replaced the original track with paving bricks, but after the 1910 races the track was still not a success. By this point the partners had invested more than $700,000 and needed one spectacular event that would bring crowds to the Speedway each year. As 1910 drew to a close a plan emerged for a 500-mile automobile race to be held at the track on Decoration Day, 1911. The Indianapolis 500 has been a Memorial Day weekend tradition ever since.

Opposite page: Farmers with their horses and wagons peddle produce on Market Street in front of the City Market, circa 1906. At the turn of the century, a large number of people bought fresh produce at the Market.

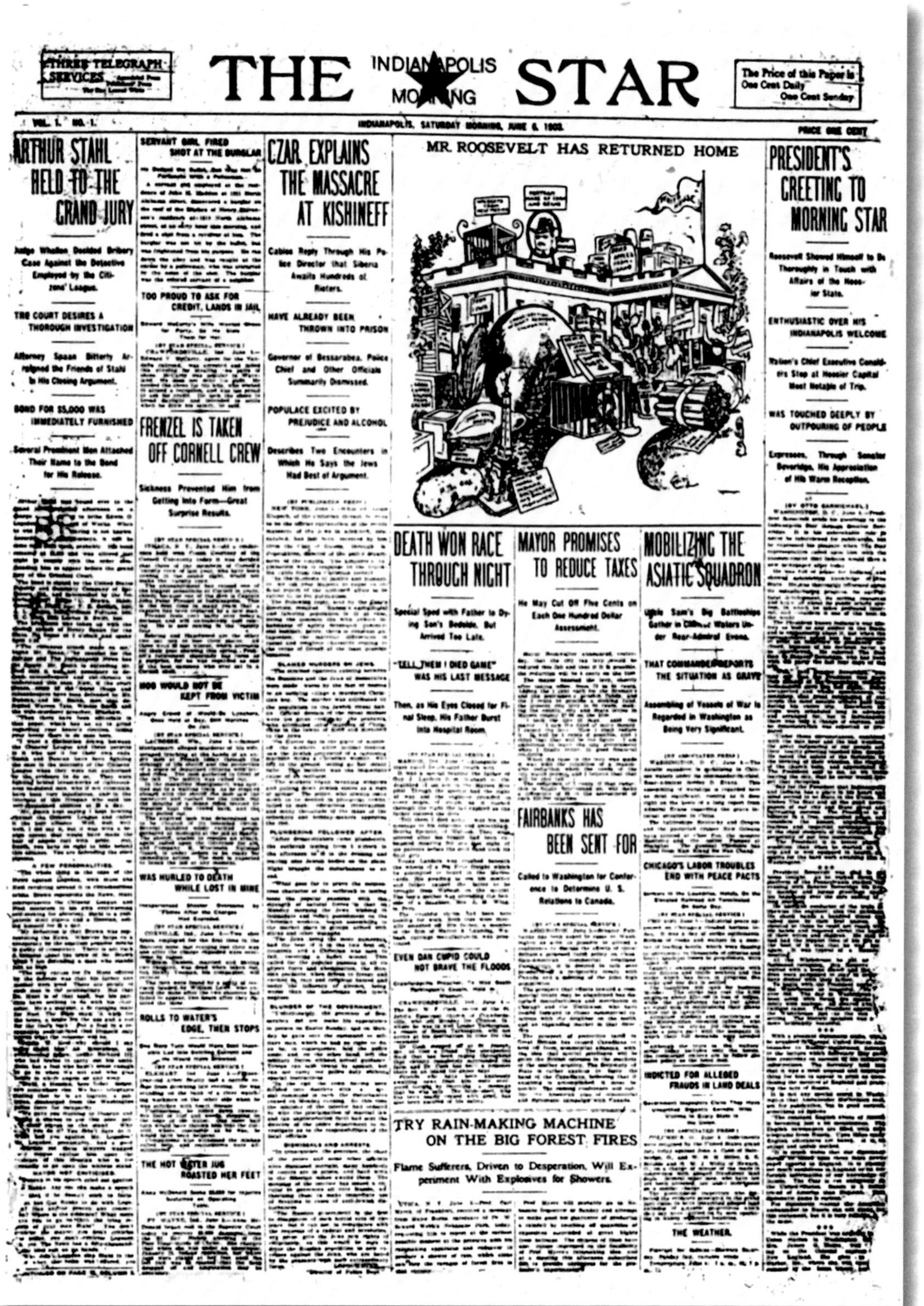

THREE TELEGRAPH SERVICES

THE INDIANAPOLIS MORNING STAR

The Price of this Paper is One Cent Daily One Cent Sunday

VOL. 1. NO. 1. INDIANAPOLIS, SATURDAY MORNING, JUNE 6, 1903. PRICE ONE CENT

ARTHUR STAHL HELD TO THE GRAND JURY

Judge Whallon Decided Bribery Case Against the Detective Employed by the Citizens' League.

THE COURT DESIRES A THOROUGH INVESTIGATION

Attorney Spaan Bitterly Arraigned the Friends of Stahl In His Closing Argument.

BOND FOR $5,000 WAS IMMEDIATELY FURNISHED

Several Prominent Men Attached Their Name to the Bond for His Release.

SERVANT GIRL FIRED SHOT AT THE BURGLAR

TOO PROUD TO ASK FOR CREDIT, LANDS IN JAIL

FRENZEL IS TAKEN OFF CORNELL CREW

Sickness Prevented Him from Getting Into Form—Great Surprise Results.

WAS HURLED TO DEATH WHILE LOST IN MINE

ROLLS TO WATER'S EDGE, THEN STOPS

THE HOT WATER JUG ROASTED HER FEET

CZAR EXPLAINS THE MASSACRE AT KISHINEFF

Cables Reply Through His Police Director that Siberia Awaits Hundreds of Rioters.

HAVE ALREADY BEEN THROWN INTO PRISON

Governor of Bessarabea, Police Chief and Other Officials Summarily Dismissed.

POPULACE EXCITED BY PREJUDICE AND ALCOHOL

Describes Two Encounters in Which He Says the Jews Had Best of Argument.

MR. ROOSEVELT HAS RETURNED HOME

DEATH WON RACE THROUGH NIGHT

Special Sped with Father to Dying Son's Bedside, But Arrived Too Late.

"TELL THEM I DIED GAME" WAS HIS LAST MESSAGE

Then, as His Eyes Closed for Final Sleep, His Father Burst Into Hospital Room.

EVEN DAN CUPID COULD NOT BRAVE THE FLOODS

MAYOR PROMISES TO REDUCE TAXES

He May Cut Off Five Cents on Each One Hundred Dollar Assessment.

FAIRBANKS HAS BEEN SENT FOR

Called to Washington for Conference to Determine U. S. Relations to Canada.

MOBILIZING THE ASIATIC SQUADRON

Uncle Sam's Big Battleships Gather in Chinese Waters Under Rear-Admiral Evans.

THAT COMMANDER REPORTS THE SITUATION AS GRAVE

Assembling of Vessels of War Is Regarded in Washington as Being Very Significant.

CHICAGO'S LABOR TROUBLES END WITH PEACE PACTS

INDICTED FOR ALLEGED FRAUDS IN LAND DEALS

THE WEATHER.

TRY RAIN-MAKING MACHINE ON THE BIG FOREST FIRES

Flame Sufferers, Driven to Desperation, Will Experiment With Explosives for Showers.

PRESIDENT'S GREETING TO MORNING STAR

Roosevelt Showed Himself to Be Thoroughly in Touch with Affairs of the Hoosier State.

ENTHUSIASTIC OVER HIS INDIANAPOLIS WELCOME

Nation's Chief Executive Considers Stop at Hoosier Capital Most Notable of Trip.

WAS TOUCHED DEEPLY BY OUTPOURING OF PEOPLE

Expresses, Through Senator Beveridge, His Appreciation of His Warm Reception.

Above: The first edition of The Star, June 6, 1903.

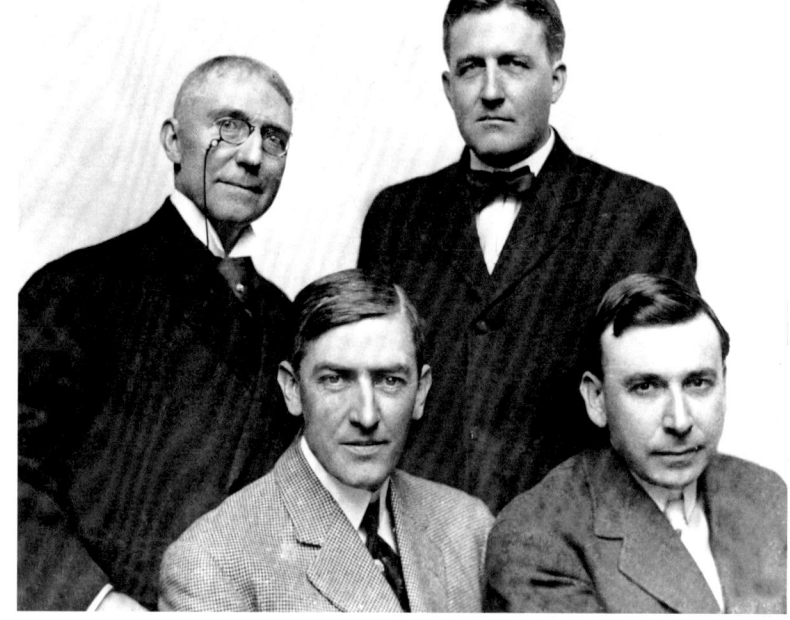

Above: Indiana's most notable authors in the first decade of the 20th century. Clockwise from top left, James Whitcomb Riley, Meredith Nicholson, Booth Tarkington and George Ade.

Below: Shortridge High School football team, champions of Indiana and Kentucky in 1900. Front row, left to right, Hall, QB; Bosler, FB; Wiley, LH; Holdson, FB; Shepheard, RT and captain. Second row, left to right, Douglas Dean, LE; Scott, Substitute End; Ward Dean, RE; Tolin, LH; Clark, RH. Back row, left to right, Gibbs, LG; Spencer, C; Rouse, Substitute Guard; Hacker, Substitute Guard; Shaw, RT; Masters, LT. The team's only defeat was to Huntington High School with three seconds left in the last game of the season on December 1.

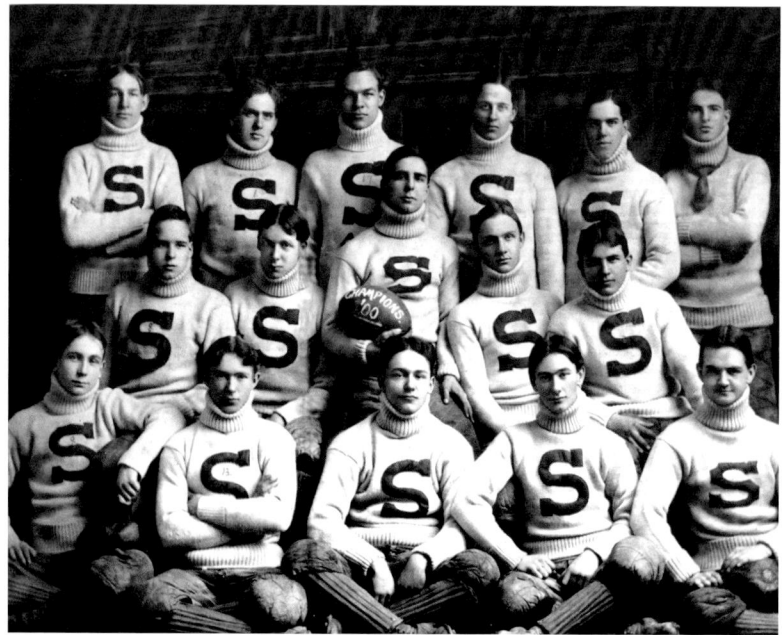

Above: A turn-of-the-century view of Indianapolis, showing the Capitol building at far left and the Downtown interurban train station and train sheds in the center. Interurban trains were intercity electric railways that connected Indianapolis with nearby small towns and all major cities in the state. Each day hundreds of trains brought commuters into the city and by 1920 Indianapolis is said to have had the largest interurban network in the U.S.

Above: A view of Indianapolis in the early 1900s, looking south on Illinois Street toward Union Station.

Left: The original William H. Block department store located on Washington Street between Meridian and Illinois streets.

Below: The Federal Building in Indianapolis, May 30, 1907. *Courtesy Indiana Historical Society, P236*

Above: Horses, street cars and pedestrians jam the intersection at Illinois and Washington streets, circa 1906. *W.H. Bass Photo Co.*

Right: A reception for President Theodore Roosevelt at the home of Vice President and Mrs. Charles Warren Fairbanks in Indianapolis, May 30, 1907. Front row, left to right, Mrs. John N. Carey, Dr. Mary A. Spink, James Whitcomb Riley, the Honorable Alber J. Beveridge, Governor J. Frank Hanly, Vice President Charles W. Fairbanks, President Theodore Roosevelt, Cornelia Cole Fairbanks, James A. Hemenway and Rear Admiral George Brown. Back row, left to right, Lucius B. Swift, William H. Armstrong, Henry Riesenberg, Meredith Nicholson, Roscoe O. Hawkins, Charles A. Bookwalter, Frank D. Stalnaker, John W. Kern, Charles Remster, the Rev. Daniel R. Lucas, Franklin Vonnegut, Dr. P. M. Rixey, Thomas Taggart, Moses G. McLain, Harry S. New, Jeremiah E. Kenney, Detective John J. Twiname, William H. H. Miller, William Loeb Jr., Secretary to the President Chauncey A. Manning, Detective Jesse Overstreet, Joseph A. Minturn, Albert B. Anderson, Addison C. Harris, Louis H. Levey and Ferdinand L. Mayer.

Right: A train bound from West Lafayette to Indianapolis carrying the Purdue football team and more than 900 students and fans collided with coal cars Oct. 31, 1903, killing 15 and injuring 50 people.

Courtesy Purdue Research Foundation

Above and left: The Indianapolis Motor Speedway's first races were held in August of 1909. Motorcycle and automobile races were run on a surface of crushed rock and tar. In September of 1909, the track began an ambitious project of resurfacing with bricks.

Above photo courtesy of the Indianapolis Motor Speedway

Growth & Tragedy

1910 - 1919

In the "Teens" Indianapolis continued to experience rapid population growth, from 233,000 in 1910 to 314,000 by the end of the decade, and although business leaders were buoyed by the city's new stature, calling it the "Queen of the Central Western States," an expanding city added new stresses to ordinary life.

As natural gas fields north of Marion County ran dry, people switched to coal. Suddenly there was a lot more coal smoke pouring from chimneys, and the new Soldiers and Sailors Monument began to look old with its patina of soot.

The city also needed sanitary sewers, and better control over the dumping of refuse. And then there was automobile exhaust. Who could blame Indianapolis author Booth Tarkington when he described urban life as a place where "the streets were thunderous; a vast energy heaved under the universal coating of dinginess?"

In his 1919 Pulitzer Prize-winning novel, *The Magnificent Ambersons*, Tarkington commented on the change brought by automobiles. "With all their speed forward they may be a step backward in civilization," he wrote. "They are here, and almost all outward things are going to be different because of what they bring."

Cars, like railroads a generation earlier, were having a major effect on the city. Indianapolis was home to the Stutz Motor Car Co., whose factory was at 10th Street and Capitol Avenue. Another sprawling plant was the home of the Cole Motor Car Co. at 730 E. Washington Street. The first running of the Indianapolis 500 was in 1911 and was raced each year afterwards except for the war years of 1917-18.

Despite the coal dust and exhaust fumes, the decade was also a time when beautification efforts in Indianapolis started to take root. Architects at the time were studying the buildings of imperial Rome, and so it was not by chance that two landmarks of this period are neo-classical in design: the Central Library (1916), 40 E. St. Clair Street, and the old City Hall (1910), later the Indiana State Museum, at 202 N. Alabama Street.

Urban planning spilled over into the parks, too. Where others saw streams such as Fall Creek as obstacles, George Kessler saw a way to create parks linked by sweeping boulevards.

The second decade of the 20th Century also brought tragedies of nature. In the spring of 1913, the city found itself waist-deep in water after 11 inches of rain fell in four days. Floodwaters broke through earthen levees along the White River, and water 4 to 10 feet deep swept over four square miles on the Westside, home to about 4,000 families. Statewide, the death toll was reported at 200. In Indianapolis, three people died and 200,000 were left homeless.

After the Great War began in Europe, German-Americans in Indianapolis found themselves under suspicion. Germans started changing their names and avoided speaking the language in public. Das Deutsche Haus at the intersection of East Michigan and New Jersey streets was re-named the Athenaeum, and the Indianapolis Public Schools board voted to end German-language teaching in all of the district's elementary schools.

In the autumn of 1918 another disaster came in the form of a global epidemic of influenza that would kill 969 city residents within a 15-week period. More than 600,000 people died nationwide and 21 million around the world.

In Indianapolis, Mayor Charles Jewett directed the police chief to begin vigorous enforcement of an anti-spitting ordinance and called for the daily fumigation and cleaning of streetcars. As local deaths and new flu cases mounted, orders prohibiting public gatherings went out to schools and movie theaters. As the death toll rose, the city Fire Department was asked to flush Downtown streets and sidewalks. Volunteers were sought to staff three Richmond casket plants that were trying to keep up with orders.

Armistice Day on Nov. 11 brought an end to the war, but added a strange twist to the epidemic. Five days later, city health officials reported a rash of new flu cases, apparently from people kissing in celebration of Germany's surrender.

Opposite page: Charles Basle, driver of car No. 17, heads for the pits with a broken crankshaft after the 46th lap of the first Indianapolis 500 in 1911.

Above, left: Ray Harroun, the first 500-mile race winner, 1911.

Above, right: Will Jones in car No. 9 was awarded 28th place in the first 500-mile Indianapolis event. His car developed steering trouble and he was forced out after 122 laps.

Right: Harry Grant with his hand on the steering wheel of his Alco/American Locomotive, which he drove in the 1911 race. On the 51st lap, the engine broke its crankshaft – he finished 33rd.

Left: Roaring around the first turn at better than 75 miles per hour, four racers duel for position in the first running of the Indianapolis 500 Mile Race May 30, 1911.

Below: Cars line up for the start of the 1911 500-Mile Race. Subsequent races started with the drivers taking one unscored and untimed lap at about 40 mph before being released to increase speed.

Above: An estimated 150,000 people crowded the streets of Downtown Indianapolis on this sweltering Fourth of July in 1911. President William Howard Taft, on his first official visit to the city, gave a speech on Monument Circle. Taft made 10 speeches in Indiana during a 32-hour period, seven more than originally planned.

Above: Charles Warren Fairbanks, who served as vice president under President Theodore Roosevelt, shared a ride with Roosevelt's successor, William Howard Taft, during Taft's visit to Indianapolis in 1911.

Below: Passengers cling to a streetcar on the Illinois Street line early in the century.

Above: The Aug. 2, 1914, edition of The Indianapolis Sunday Star announced the beginning of World War I.

Chapter Two ~ 1910–1919

Opposite Page: The Indiana State Fairgrounds moved to its current location in the late 1800s. By 1908, the racetrack, coliseum and exhibition buildings had been built; however, the modern day problem of parking was not yet addressed (left).

Right: The grand cattle cavalcade at the State Fairgrounds, circa 1915.

Below: James Whitcomb Riley, the "children's poet," is shown surrounded by youngsters at his home in Indianapolis shortly before his death in 1916.

Above: Madame C.J. Walker (second from left), along with (left to right) George Knox, Freeman B. Ransom, Booker T. Washington, Alexander Manning, Dr. Joseph Ward, R. W. Bullock, and Thomas A. Taylor attended the Senate Avenue Young Men's Christian Association dedication in 1913. *Courtesy Madam C. J. Walker Collection, Indiana Historical Society Library*

Chapter Two ~ 1910-1919

Above: Five modes of transportation can be seen looking northwest toward Downtown from the Virginia Avenue viaduct in 1914. Pedestrians used a brick sidewalk between the Pennsylvania Railroad yard and the inclined street, on which a lone motorcar passes a horse and wagon and a streetcar headed to or from Shelby Street.

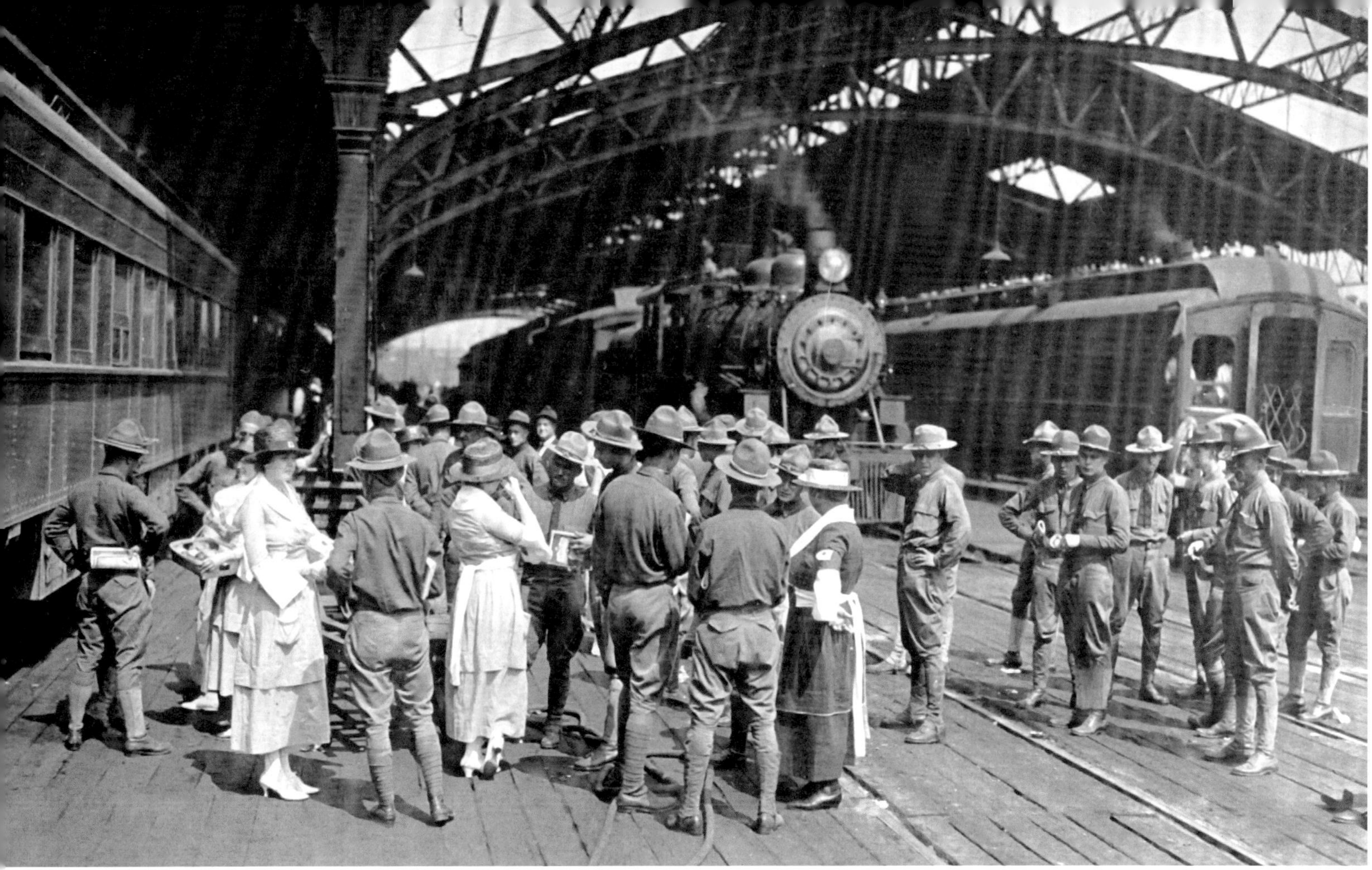

Left: World War I doughboys are served refreshments at the Indianapolis Union Station by Red Cross Volunteers.

Below, left: Soldiers drill at Fort Harrison, circa 1917.

Below, right: Indiana recruits pass through a wooden chute on Sept. 9, 1917, as they are processed to enter military service. World War I had been raging in Europe for three years, but the United States did not declare war on Germany until April 1917. The first Selective Service Draft Act was passed in May of that year, requiring all American men between the ages of 21 and 30 to register. During that summer, American troops began pouring into France at the rate of 50,000 a month.

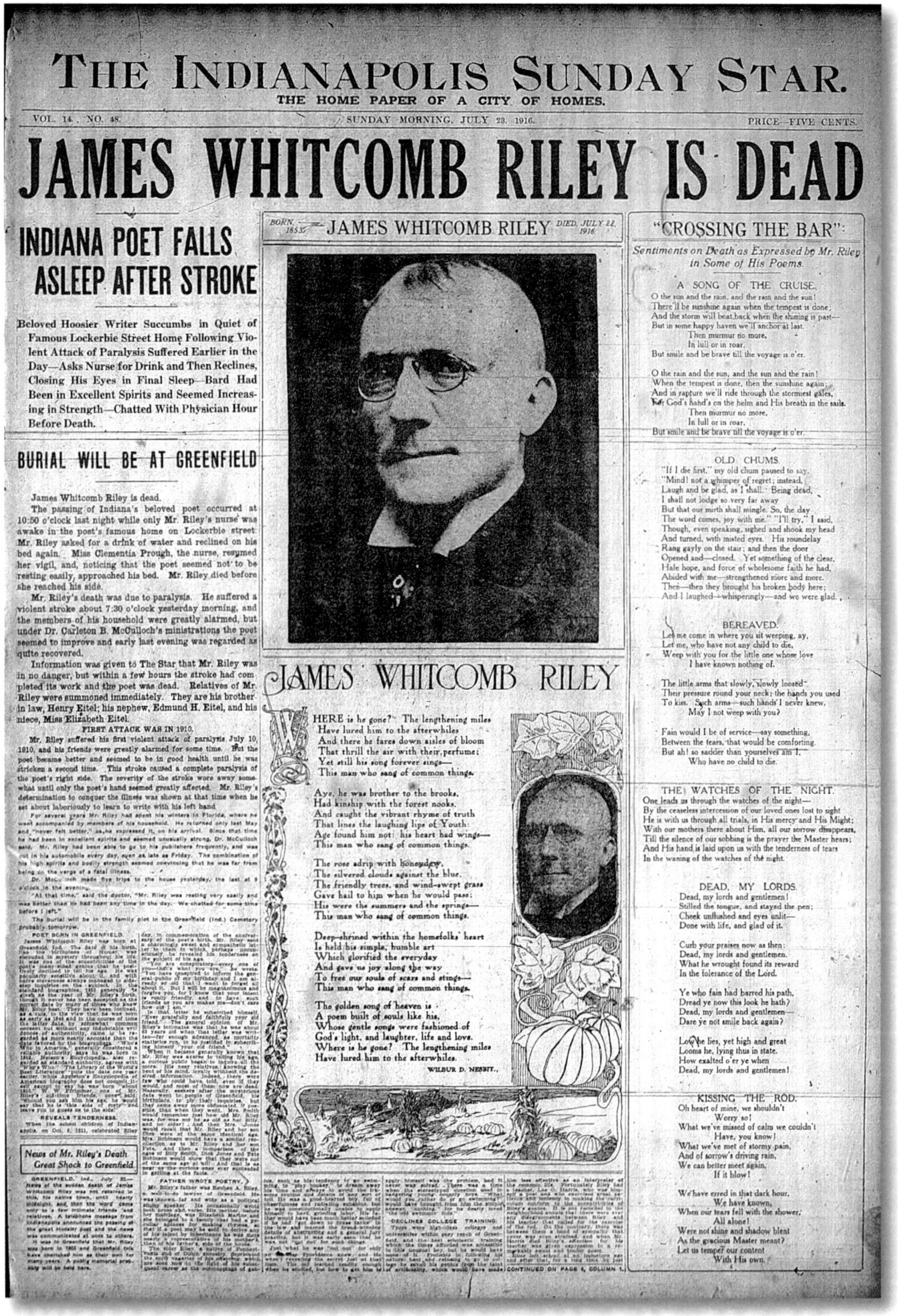

Above: The July 23, 1916, edition of The Indianapolis Sunday Star.

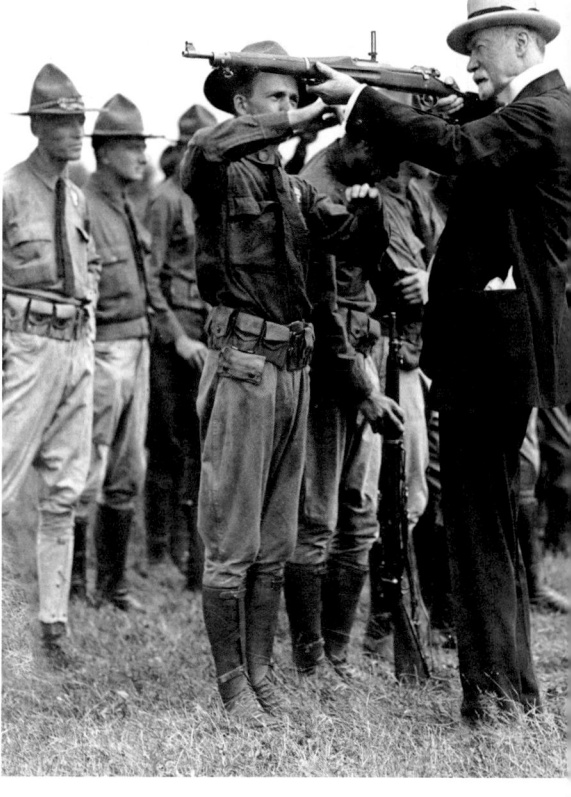

Right and below: Charles Warren Fairbanks, a former U.S. Senator and vice-president under Theodore Roosevelt (1905-1909), was a frequent visitor to Fort Benjamin Harrison during training periods and is shown here examining the sight of a rifle in 1917. The photo below shows Fairbanks' funeral procession to the Statehouse on June 6, 1918. Walking behind the casket are Indiana Gov. James P. Goodrich and Indianapolis Mayor Charles W. Jewett.

Above: Indianapolis defense workers celebrate the news that Germany had agreed to an armistice on Nov. 11, 1918, bringing an end to the horror and destruction of World War I. This photo, shot in the first block of Kentucky Avenue, looks south from near Washington Street. "The Great War," which began in July 1914, took the lives of nearly 10 million troops. The United States lost 116,516, including nearly 3,400 Hoosiers.

Chapter Two ~ 1910-1919

Above: Thousands cheered as returning soldiers, sailors and Marines paraded through the heart of Downtown on May 7, 1919. A replica of Paris' Arc de Triomphe on Monument Circle was erected to celebrate the Armistice of Nov. 11, 1918.

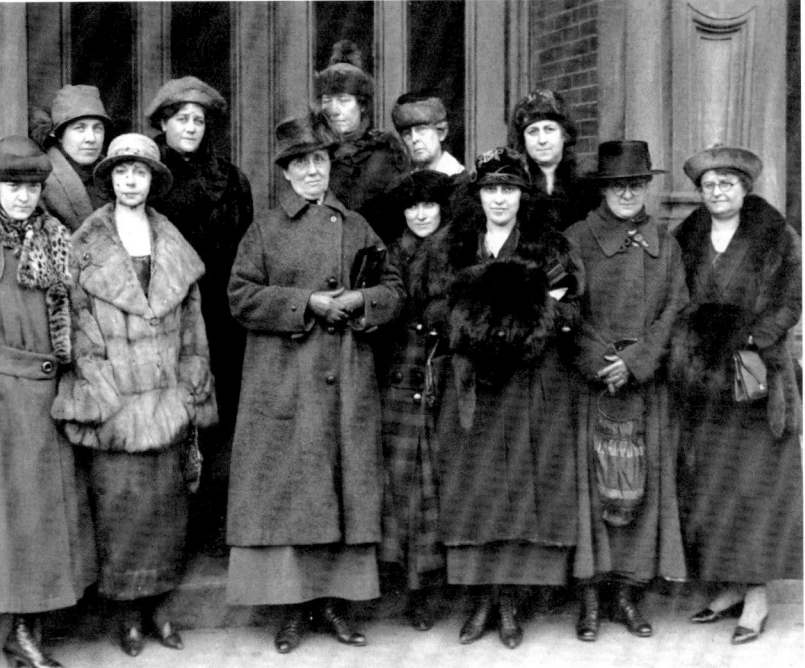

Right: In January 1919, members of the Women's Franchise League of Indiana petitioned for suffrage at the Indiana Statehouse. During a 20-year period, fewer than 10 women's suffrage bills were proposed to the Indiana General Assembly, and all either were rejected or ignored. Indiana ratified the 19th Amendment to the Constitution, which granted women the right to vote, in a special session of the General Assembly on Jan. 16, 1920. Congress ratified it Aug. 18, 1920.

Above: Interior of the Circle Theatre, circa 1919.

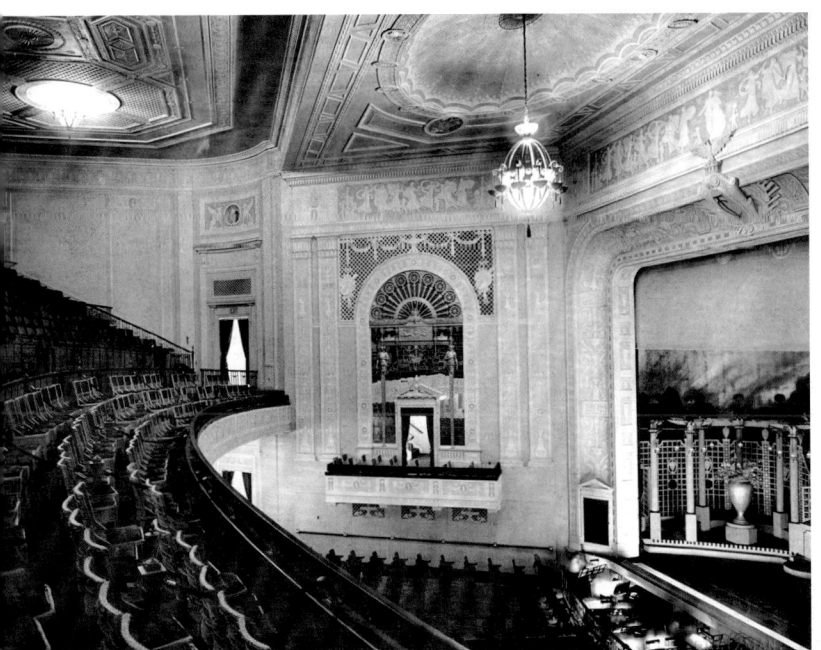

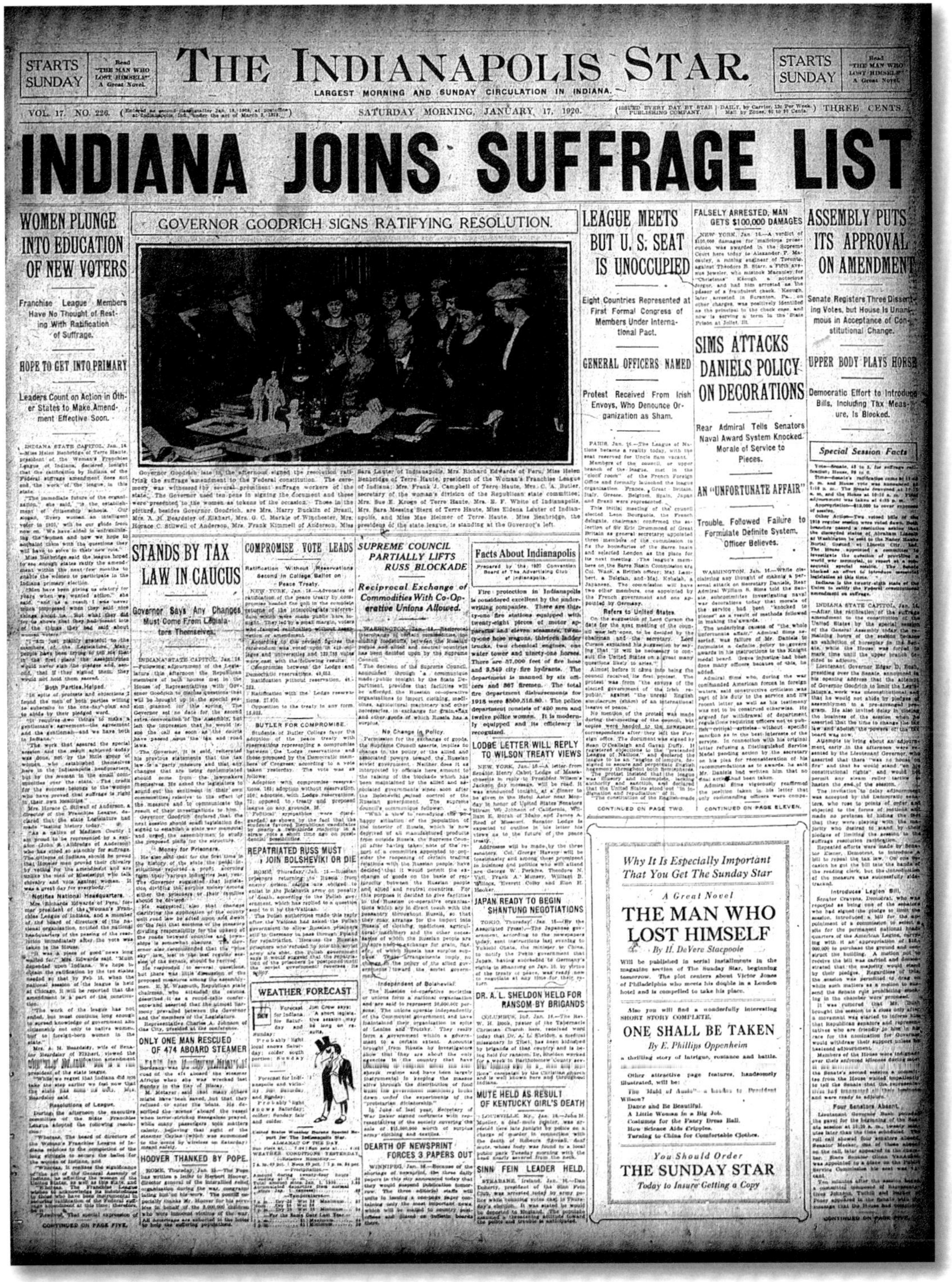

STARTS SUNDAY "THE MAN WHO LOST HIMSELF" A Great Novel.

THE INDIANAPOLIS STAR.

LARGEST MORNING AND SUNDAY CIRCULATION IN INDIANA.

VOL. 17. NO. 226. SATURDAY MORNING, JANUARY 17, 1920. THREE CENTS.

INDIANA JOINS SUFFRAGE LIST

WOMEN PLUNGE INTO EDUCATION OF NEW VOTERS

Franchise League Members Have No Thought of Resting With Ratification of Suffrage.

HOPE TO GET INTO PRIMARY

Leaders Count on Action in Other States to Make Amendment Effective Soon.

GOVERNOR GOODRICH SIGNS RATIFYING RESOLUTION.

LEAGUE MEETS BUT U. S. SEAT IS UNOCCUPIED

Eight Countries Represented at First Formal Congress of Members Under International Pact.

GENERAL OFFICERS NAMED

Protest Received From Irish Envoys, Who Denounce Organization as Sham.

FALSELY ARRESTED, MAN GETS $100,000 DAMAGES

SIMS ATTACKS DANIELS POLICY ON DECORATIONS

Rear Admiral Tells Senators Naval Award System Knocked Morale of Service to Pieces.

AN "UNFORTUNATE AFFAIR"

Trouble, Followed Failure to Formulate Definite System, Officer Believes.

ASSEMBLY PUTS ITS APPROVAL ON AMENDMENT

Senate Registers Three Dissenting Votes, but House Is Unanimous in Acceptance of Constitutional Change.

UPPER BODY PLAYS HORSE

Democratic Effort to Introduce Bills, Including Tax Measure, Is Blocked.

Special Session Facts

STANDS BY TAX LAW IN CAUCUS

Governor Says Any Changes Must Come From Legislators Themselves.

COMPROMISE VOTE LEADS

SUPREME COUNCIL PARTIALLY LIFTS RUSS BLOCKADE

Reciprocal Exchange of Commodities With Co-Operative Unions Allowed.

Facts About Indianapolis

LODGE LETTER WILL REPLY TO WILSON TREATY VIEWS

REPATRIATED RUSS MUST JOIN BOLSHEVIKI OR DIE

ONLY ONE MAN RESCUED OF 474 ABOARD STEAMER

HOOVER THANKED BY POPE.

WEATHER FORECAST

JAPAN READY TO BEGIN SHANTUNG NEGOTIATIONS

DR. A. L. SHELDON HELD FOR RANSOM BY BRIGANDS

MUTE HELD AS RESULT OF KENTUCKY GIRL'S DEATH

SINN FEIN LEADER HELD.

DEARTH OF NEWSPRINT FORCES 3 PAPERS OUT

Why It Is Especially Important That You Get The Sunday Star

A Great Novel

THE MAN WHO LOST HIMSELF

By H. DeVere Stacpoole

ONE SHALL BE TAKEN

By E. Phillips Oppenheim

You Should Order

THE SUNDAY STAR

Today to Insure Getting a Copy

CONTINUED ON PAGE FIVE.

CONTINUED ON PAGE TWO.

CONTINUED ON PAGE ELEVEN.

Above: The Jan. 17, 1920, edition of The Indianapolis Star.

Era of Change, Shame
1920 - 1929

The decade of the 1920s was a grand period in Indianapolis history – for the buildings. For people it was less gracious, especially if you were black or Catholic or if you spoke with a foreign accent. This was the decade of the Ku Klux Klan.

But first, the buildings.

Around the Circle, older buildings vanished as a new generation took their place — the Guarantee (1922) and Test (1925) on the southwest quadrant, and the Columbia Club (1924-25) on the northeast quadrant.

To entice the American Legion to pick Indianapolis as its national headquarters, the city agreed to build a war memorial and office building. It set about preparing a five-block site between Pennsylvania and Meridian streets, with Central Library and the U.S. Courthouse serving as bookends to the north and south.

Many of today's landmarks were completed between 1926 and 1929. Among them: the Scottish Rite Cathedral, the Indiana Theatre, the Madame Walker Building and several buildings at the state fairgrounds. Three city high schools also were built in the 1920s — Shortridge, Crispus Attucks and Cathedral's former home on North Meridian Street.

Farther out, Butler University moved to its current campus from Irvington, and Jordan Hall and Hinkle Fieldhouse were built in 1928.

The Gothic-style Tabernacle Presbyterian Church (1923) was built at 34th Street and Central Avenue, and St. Joan of Arc Catholic Church (1929) went up at 42nd and Central.

But history is more about people than buildings, and people are generally less grand than the landmarks they erect. Indiana in the 1920s also saw a boom in membership in the Ku Klux Klan.

In the aftermath of a world war, people remained suspicious of anything foreign. Indianapolis, a city that prided itself on being 100 percent American, may have been ripe for the Klan's warped message. Certainly the city was unlucky that the Klan's most potent messenger of the time chose to make Indianapolis his home base.

D. C. Stephenson, a salesman from Oklahoma, arrived in Evansville and quickly became involved in the growing Klan movement in Indiana. He re-located to Indianapolis in 1922 and was named Grand Dragon of Indiana and 22 other states.

In the May primary of 1924, the KKK emerged as the dominant party, and on May 24, an estimated 25,000 Klansmen, women and children gathered at the State Fairgrounds. Later the same day, Klan members assembled at 14th Street and Capitol Avenue for a parade. Most of the marchers wore masks, while some wore hoods and robes. The marchers numbered some 6,500, according to news reports of the time, while a crowd of 75,000 to 100,000 lined the streets and filled the windows of buildings along the march route.

For much of the 1920s the Klan would be the dominant force in Indianapolis politics. Candidates openly supported by the Klan won the mayor's office, the City Council and the Board of School Commissioners in 1925. Klan-supported candidates also controlled the state legislature and governor's office.

The Klan's power began to decline after Stephenson was convicted of murder in 1925, and several Klan members were forced out of office by a series of scandals.

Into this unwelcome atmosphere, blacks from the South continued to migrate. During the 1920s the African-American population in the city grew from 34,678 to 43,967. But hardening segregation kept most of them within a few neighborhoods that lay to the north and west of Downtown.

When middle-class blacks sought better housing outside these areas, they ran into a number of roadblocks. In 1926, the City Council adopted an ordinance requiring blacks to first get the permission of white residents before moving onto a block. It was declared unconstitutional, but efforts to restrict housing choices for blacks continued.

In the midst of this repression, Indiana Avenue blossomed as a town within a town, a place where black residents ran their own groceries, bakeries, hardware and clothing stores. There were professional offices next to hole-in-the-wall dance clubs, and jazz joints where many of the great musicians of that era came to play. The Madame Walker Theatre opened in 1927 on Indiana Avenue at North and West streets. Named for Madame C.J. Walker, who had built her fortune selling cosmetics made for black women, the Walker Building and its Coffee Pot restaurant became the centerpiece of life on the Avenue.

Also in 1927, Attucks High School opened as the segregated school for blacks. Despite the unfairness of its purpose, segregation produced a concentration of talent at Attucks that became legendary in the black community long after the barriers had fallen. Although not as grand architecturally as some of the other buildings of the 1920s, Attucks has come to be regarded by many as one of the most historically significant landmarks in the city.

Opposite page: The Grand Army of the Republic, an organization of Civil War veterans, held several reunions in Indianapolis, such as this one in September 1920.

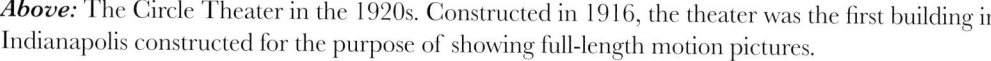

Above: The Circle Theater in the 1920s. Constructed in 1916, the theater was the first building in Indianapolis constructed for the purpose of showing full-length motion pictures.

Right: Fort Benjamin Harrison was used as an officer training camp and training facility for medical and engineering specialists. Circa March 1920.

Above: Cattle judging at the Indiana State Fair, circa 1920.

Right: Construction of the Indiana World War Memorial plaza begins in 1926.

Below: Indianapolis ABC's Negro National League baseball team, circa 1922.

Above: The William H. Block Company at the corner of Illinois and Market Street in 1929.

Left: Racing fans headed for the Indianapolis Motor Speedway, May 30, 1923. The 1923 race marked a turning point at the Speedway: The practice of having mechanics ride in the cars became a thing of the past. Tommy Milton, became the first two-time winner at the race.

Above: Methodist Episcopal Hospital was built in 1908 at Capitol Avenue and 16th Street. An expansion project was completed in 1916, which added 250 beds, making it the largest hospital in the state.

Right: The English Hotel and Opera House circa 1923. Encompassing the northwest quadrant of the Circle, the hotel and opera house rivaled each other in grandeur and opulence. The theater boasted such performers as Sarah Bernhardt and Laurence Olivier. The structure was demolished in 1948.

Above: American Legion Headquarters at the corner of Meridian and St. Clair streets in 1925.

Below: The Claypool Court built in 1903 at the corner of Illinois and Washington streets. The hotel was demolished in 1969 after a fire forced its closing in 1967.

Above: The Nov. 15, 1925 edition of The Indianapolis Sunday Star. The Grand Dragon of the Ku Klux Klan in Indiana received a life sentence for his role in the rape and murder of Madge Oberholtzer. While in prison, Stephenson revealed his involvement in state politics, ending the careers of Governor Ed Jackson and Indianapolis Mayor John Duvall.

Above: The May 22, 1927 edition of The Indianapolis Sunday Star heralds the cross-Atlantic flight of Charles Lindbergh.

Above: Butler Fieldhouse, constructed in 1928, is one the nation's oldest college basketball arenas. It was renamed Hinkle Fieldhouse in 1965 after legendary Butler Coach Tony Hinkle. While "Hoosier Hysteria" swept through Indiana during the month of March, the Fieldhouse was the final destination for high school basketball teams seeking a state championship.

Below: The Indianapolis Children's Museum, shown here in 1929, was located in the home of museum founder Mary Stewart Carey at 1150 N. Meridian Street. The museum moved to it's current location of 3000 N. Meridian Street in 1946 and has since become one of the largest children's museums in the world.

Left and above: Completed in 1929, the Scottish Rite Cathedral is the home of the Scottish Rite Valley of Indianapolis. It is the largest building in the world dedicated exclusively to Scottish Rite Freemasonry and was placed on the National Register of Historic Places in 1983.

Below: The Capitol Theater and Indiana Theater were side by side on Washington Street, circa 1929.

Surviving the Depression
1930 - 1939

Like the rest of America, Indianapolis spent most of the 1930s in the grip of the Great Depression. Business had been good prior to the stock market crash in October 1929. But by early 1930, nearly 17,000 people, or 9.3 percent of Indianapolis' work force, needed a job. By 1933, the unemployment rate was 37 percent.

The city had experienced hard times before, but nothing like this. Life savings disappeared overnight as banks closed, and before people could catch their breath, they were out of work.

A list of bank closings in 1930 read like a state directory: Monon, Whitestown, North Liberty, Kirklin, Plymouth, Monticello, Gary, East Chicago, Kewanna and Argos were among 19 Indiana cities and towns where a bank closed in 1930. In Indianapolis, 10 banks failed from 1927 to 1933.

In February 1930, business leaders formed a commission "to study and act for the stabilization of employment in Indianapolis."

In 1932, a shantytown of makeshift homes, made out of whatever was handy, appeared on the city's Near Westside near White River.

During the early years of the Depression, Indiana Gov. Harry Leslie, like other state and national leaders, was reluctant to intervene.

In 1931, the Democrats controlled the Indiana House, while the Republicans held the Senate and the governor's office. The divided legislature passed the first old-age pension act in the state's history, but Gov. Leslie vetoed the measure.

By 1932, people were ready for a change. Leading the way in Indiana was Paul V. McNutt. The handsome, silver-haired dean of the Indiana University School of Law was swept into the governor's office in a Democratic Party landslide in the 1932 elections that also gave him overwhelming majorities in both chambers of the Legislature.

McNutt came into office two months prior to the new president, Franklin Delano Roosevelt, and in his inaugural address, McNutt anticipated much of FDR's message, comparing the Depression to war and urging people not to panic out of fear for the future.

McNutt's administration was perhaps the most activist of any governor Hoosiers could remember. Previous governors certainly had ideas and plans, but they left it up to legislators to introduce bills.

McNutt's team set up a "bill factory" at the Indianapolis Athletic Club, where legislative proposals were crafted. The new administration had floor leaders in both houses to make sure nothing went wrong once the legislation was introduced.

With a 91-9 majority in the House and a 43-7 majority in the Senate, not much did go wrong. McNutt launched a series of legislative initiatives ranging from poor relief to reorganizing state government.

In another parallel to FDR, McNutt used radio to hold a series of Sunday evening talks to comfort the public.

Although Indianapolis got its first radio station in 1921, it was in the 1930s that the new medium became widely popular – and in hard times it was free entertainment.

Prizefights were broadcast from the Naval Armory, Fort Benjamin Harrison and the old Washington Street ballpark, with Ralph "Cauliflower" Elvin as announcer.

Local radio personalities of the day included Ken Ellington and Durward Kirby of WFBM. Kirby went on to national fame in both radio and television. The station also had a program featuring Bob and Gayle Sherwood as they sailed above the city in a hot-air balloon.

For a dime, one could escape the harsh realities of the time for four hours of entertainment — a double feature, cartoons and a newsreel — at one of the city's many movie houses.

During the summer of 1934, Hoosiers could also find entertainment and adventure in news reports about Indianapolis native John Dillinger, the famous bank robber who had been declared Public Enemy Number One by FBI Director J. Edgar Hoover. Dillinger shot his way out of repeated attempts to capture him but was eventually betrayed by the famous "woman in red" in a Chicago movie theater and was gunned down in a shootout.

Dillinger's funeral in Maywood, just south of Indianapolis, drew a crowd of the curious. His grave at Crown Hill Cemetery became a tourist attraction.

Opposite page: The Indianapolis Star and the Salvation Army provided ice blocks through donations to The Penny Ice Fund during the 1930's and '40's. The fund tried to ensure that no family went through the summer without ice to provide a cool drink or to safeguard food supplies.

Above: Longacre Recreation Park's kidney-shaped pool made the Southside facility one of the city's most popular recreation centers. It was first developed by attorney Edward E. Thompson in the early 1920s. He sold out to Rufus Dodrill Jr., whose family operated it from 1948 to 1972. Up to 7,500 people crammed into the park on a hot Sunday. Photo circa 1930.

Below: When the Indianapolis Municipal Airport opened in 1931 it was the first airport in the Midwest to have concrete runways. The field was renamed Weir Cook Municipal Airport on March 28, 1944, in honor of H. Weir Cook, a World War II pilot from Indiana. In 1976, the field was renamed Indianapolis International Airport.

Above: Charles Lindbergh made a brief stop at Stout field on Indianapolis' southwestside in 1930.

Above: The Bijou Theater, circa 1930. *Courtesy Bass Photo Collection, (217080-F), Indiana Historical Society*

Left: Tomlinson Hall was used as a grand hall for citizens and city authorities. Commissioned by the widow of druggist Stephen D. Tomlinson in 1883, the hall featured an auditorium, offices and marketplace. It served as a shelter and site of many political rallies. Tomlinson Hall was destroyed by fire in 1958, leaving only a doorway arch, which still stands today in the City Market courtyard.

Below: Pennsylvania Street with the Palace Theater at left. *Courtesy Bass Photo Collection, (216341-F), Indiana Historical Society*

Right and far right: New York Gov. Franklin D. Roosevelt, the Democratic presidential candidate, speaks to a crowd of nearly 60,000 from the balcony of the English Opera House on Oct. 20, 1932. It was the midst of the Great Depression and Roosevelt won by a landslide over incumbent Herbert Hoover, whom many voters blamed for the hard times that followed the stock market crash of 1929. During his 12 years in office, FDR visited Indianapolis twice. On Sept. 5, 1936, he opened the Indiana State Fair, and on May 13, 1937, the president stopped briefly to meet with postmaster general and Democratic National Chairman James A. Farley.

Above: The July 23, 1934, edition of The Indianapolis Star announces the slaying of outlaw John Dillenger.

Left: Hoosier outlaw John Dillinger, shown here posing with his guns around 1933, was so successful at robbing banks and evading capture that FBI Director J. Edgar Hoover named him "Public Enemy Number One." *Courtesy Indiana Historical Society*

Center and below: After Dillinger was gunned down in 1934, his body was brought back to his hometown of Mooresville, just southwest of Indianapolis, where thousands gathered to view the famous outlaw's body. Dillinger's funeral was at the home of his sister, Audrey Hancock, in Maywood, and he was buried in Crown Hill Cemetery in Indianapolis. In 1992 cemetery officials said Dillinger's tombstone had been replaced three times because of souvenir-seekers chipping pieces of it away.

Above: On Oct. 17, 1935, the Indianapolis Fire Department rolled out a new pumper truck made entirely by the fire department repair shop. During the Depression, many fire departments built their own trucks. A new one would have cost nearly $14,000, but this truck was built for just $6,500. It remained in service until 1955.

Above: Author and playwright Booth Tarkington used his hometown of Indianapolis as the backdrop for many of his novels. Tarkington won Pulitzer Prizes for *The Magnificent Ambersons* and *Alice Adams*.

Right: This 1935 slum in Indianapolis was known as Curtisville Bottom, referring to President Herbert Hoover's vice president, Charles Curtis. During the Great Depression, Indianapolis, like most cities in America, had settlements of shacks where unemployed families lived. This view is from Washington Street looking south.

Above: The Sept. 6, 1936, edition of The Indianapolis Sunday Star.

Above: Indianapolis Star Copy Desk, 1936.

Below: Goalie Jimmy Franks (left) and center Don Deacon, two of the players for the new Indianapolis Capitals, pose for a picture on the ice before the team made its home debut on Nov. 10, 1939, at the Fairgrounds Coliseum. The Capitals, owned by the Detroit Red Wings, were members of the International-American Hockey League. They played in Indianapolis until 1952 and again in the fall of 1963. In November 1963, three weeks into the regular season, the team was moved to Cincinnati, Ohio, in the aftermath of the Coliseum explosion.

Above: Saints Peter and Paul Cathedral at the southeast corner of 14th and Meridian streets, circa 1937.

Below: Northeast corner of Illinois and Market streets, Sept. 27, 1939.

Above: The May 31, 1936, edition of The Indianapolis Sunday Star.

Chapter Four ~ 1930-1939

UNITED WE STOOD
1940 - 1949

On Dec. 10, 1941, World War II came home to Indianapolis. It came in the form of a photo on the front page of The Indianapolis Star showing a confident-looking young man, Robert Allen, age 21. He was the first Hoosier reported killed in the Japanese attack on Pearl Harbor.

Such pictures soon became a staple in Indiana newspapers. By the time the last soldier had been accounted for, 300,000 Hoosiers had served in the war and more than 10,000 had died.

The city's mettle had been tested before – by the previous war, by flood, epidemic and the lingering Depression – and through it all, people seemed able to hold onto the belief that there was a better future, no matter how bleak the moment.

At least the war blew away the cobwebs of the Depression, as thousands of jobs were created. Industry went into overdrive. Allison churned out airplane engines, Studebaker produced trucks, Eli Lilly and Co. supplied blood plasma and RCA turned out proximity fuses.

Before Pearl Harbor, Indiana was considered among the most isolationist states in the nation. A Gallup Poll in May 1941 showed only 15 percent of Hoosiers favored the United States' entry into the war. But after Pearl Harbor, Indianapolis reacted as if the Japanese had attacked Monument Circle.

From the pages of The Star on Dec. 8, 1941: "Indianapolis unfurled hundreds of American flags to gray and cold December skies yesterday, determined to keep the Stars and Stripes flying as a symbol of Hoosier and National unity as the country declared war on Japan."

Hundreds of young men showed up at the Navy recruiting office, thinking the Navy offered the quickest opportunity to strike back at the Japanese.

"They put aside their high school and college textbooks, their mechanic's tools, their ledgers, their briefcases and their truck driver's caps; they left their schools and their farms and their jobs behind counters," Mary Bostwick wrote in The Star.

As the young men went off to war, those left behind had to deal with rationing. They stood in line for ration books and then stood in line again to buy what scarce commodities were available. But even standing in line seemed patriotic.

Even high school students found that war changed the type of math problems they had to solve. Instead of the usual problems, students were confronted with navigation, surveying and gunnery questions.

And suddenly high school machine shop classes that seemed pointless during the Depression, since there were no jobs, took on a new urgency. The students were learning to work in defense plants. One local defense plant was the Naval Ordinance Plant (later known as Naval Avionics), which manufactured the Norden bombsight, which allowed American bombers to strike targets from high altitudes.

As more and more men were taken away, a labor shortage was created, and women and blacks stepped into the breach, setting the stage for the civil rights and women's rights movements of the 1960s. Such moves caused people to confront racial issues and create day-care centers for children whose mothers were now working.

Women had been in the work force before the war, but of the 250,000 women working outside the home in Indiana in 1940, most had clerical or service positions. The war changed that. The number of Hoosier working women jumped to 390,000 by 1943. By the end of 1943, women made up one-third of the factory workers in the state.

The Indianapolis Star, the city's only morning newspaper, had been owned and operated by John Shaffer since 1908. But in 1943, Shaffer died and The Star was up for sale. Although the suitors included several nationally known publishers, in the end the winning bidder was a small-town Indiana publisher named Eugene C. Pulliam, who took ownership of The Star in 1944.

Pulliam already owned papers in Franklin and Lebanon and, in 1948, he also bought The Indianapolis News. It was the beginning of a newspaper dynasty that would last half a century.

Just days before the war ended there was a disaster at sea. The U.S.S. Indianapolis, a heavy cruiser with more than 1,100 men on board, was sunk by Japanese torpedoes while on its way back to the Philippines after delivering components for the atomic bomb. Although some 900 men survived the initial attack, they floated for five days in the shark infested waters. When help finally arrived, only 317 men were alive.

Opposite page: VJ Day on Monument Circle, August 1945.

Above: Elwood native, Wendell Willkie accepts the 1940 Republican presidential nomination. Willkie lost the election to Franklin D. Roosevelt by 5 million votes.

Right: Willkie addresses the crowd from the front of the English Hotel on Monument Circle. October 1940.

Above: Lieutenant Lloyd R. Stewart swears in Marion County draftees Nov. 20, 1940. Front row, left to right, Julius Galbreath, William Wendell Frierson, Alfred Maxey, Earl Leo Fultz, Samuel Richards White, Thomas Roscoe Armstrong, Charles Edward Buell and Robert Petticord Hadley. Back row, Robert Stanley Hill, Lawrence Adams, James Robert McLeod, Harold Edwards Bowman and Leslie Arvel Troxell.

Above: Mrs. Dorothy Knop beats a large pan with a potato masher to attract the attention of hungry fair workers and concession operators to the lunch tent operated at the Indiana State Fair by the Garfield Park Evangelical Reformed Church in 1940.

Above: The Dec. 8, 1941, edition of The Indianapolis Star.

Chapter Five ~ 1940-1949

Above: The U.S.S. Indianapolis was torpedoed by a Japanese submarine on July 30, 1945, only days before the end of WWII. Nearly 1,200 men were on the ship and those who survived the attack were stranded in shark-infested waters for five days. When help finally arrived, only 317 men were still alive. *Official U.S. Navy photo*

Below: Sacramento Club float in the Navy Booster Day parade, February 1942. The club was formed by wives, mothers and other relatives of Indiana naval reservists called to active duty aboard the gunboat Sacramento during World War II.

Above: Actress Carole Lombard, a Fort Wayne native, thanks Melvin Dennis Loeb, 5-year-old son of Mrs. Alice Loeb, as he purchases a $25 war bond, January 1942. Lombard sold more than $2 million in bonds at the rally, a sales record, then caught an early flight out of Indianapolis the next morning. Lombard was killed when her plane crashed 20 miles west of Las Vegas while en route to Hollywood.

Left: Lieutenant Neil C. Russell (far right), Office of Naval Officer Procurement, and Ensign Mary Richmond (second from right), of the WAVES, administer the oath to new recruits (left to right) Dorotha Overstreet, Bernice H. G. Hamilton, Ruth L. Allen, Mary Janet Plummer, Janet Fabe and France Snodgrass, Dec. 30, 1942.

Right: Civil Defense display at the Murat Theater, circa 1942. *Courtesy Bass Photo Collection, (258480), Indiana Historical Society*

Below: Enlistees march in the Navy Booster parade, February 1942. In the background is The Indianapolis Star building.

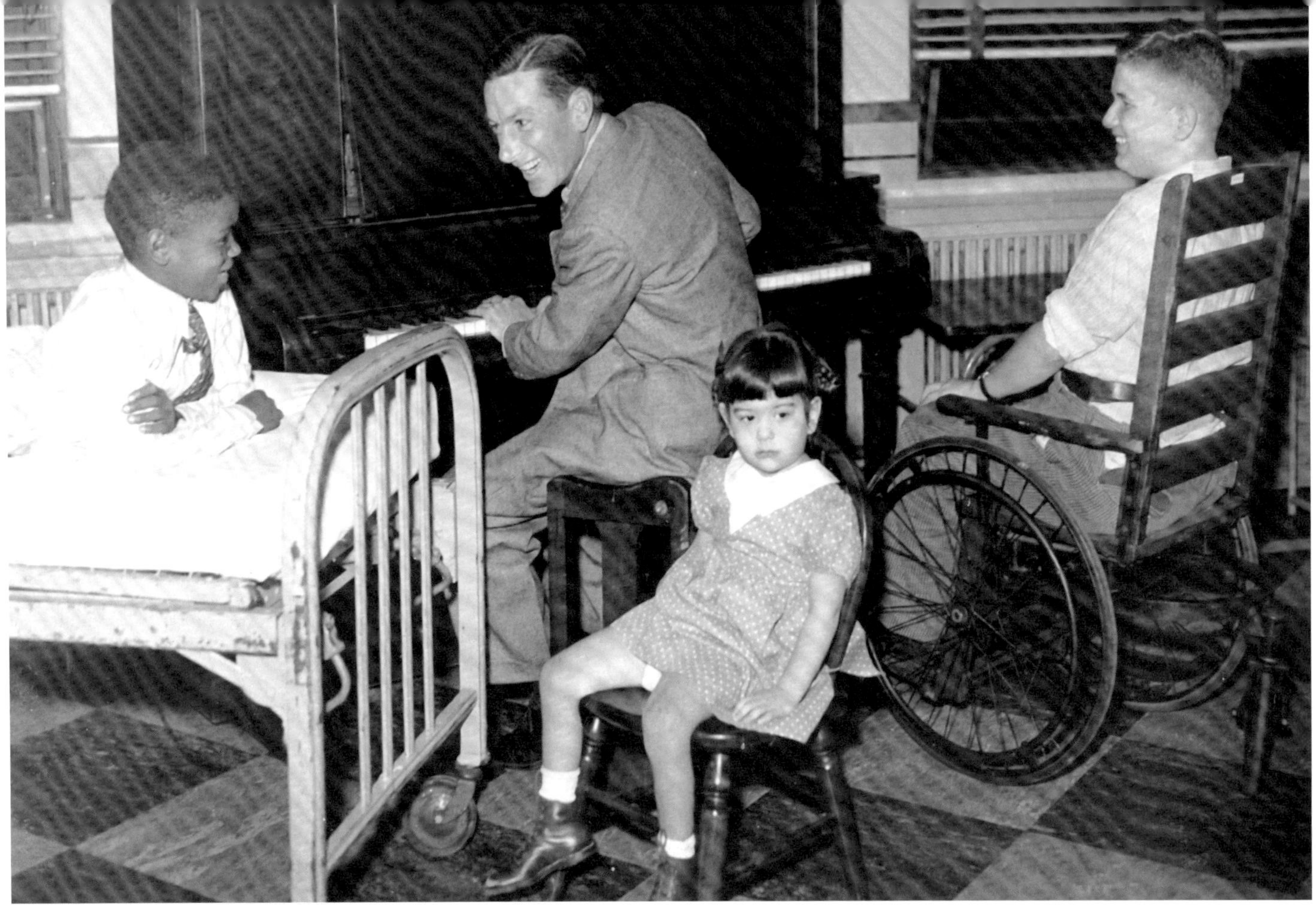

Right: Hoosier composer and singer Hoagy Carmichael performs several tunes on Jan. 29, 1942, for young patients at James Whitcomb Riley Hospital. Carmichael, who wrote songs such as "Star Dust" and "Georgia On My Mind," was in Indianapolis to perform the following day at Butler Fieldhouse.

Below: The inaugural ride on the "Victory Express" at Riverside Park on May 13, 1942. The train offered visitors sightseeing tours through the park. Riverside Park, built in 1903 along the White River at West 30th Street, resembled New York's Coney Island, with boat rides and "Shoot the Chutes" waterslide and "The Flash" rollercoaster. It's popularity peaked during World War II, but declined steadily afterwards and the park was closed in 1970.

Above: The 44th Women's Army Auxiliary Corps at noon dinner in the mess hall at Camp Atterbury, March 1943. Atterbury, located near Edinburgh in Johnson County, opened in 1942 and served as a training facility for nearly 275,000 soldiers during World War II. The camp also was the site of the 2,700-bed Wakeman General Hospital, which specialized in reconstructive plastic surgery for wounded soldiers, and an internment camp for more than 15,000 captured Italian and German troops. Since World War II the camp has served as a Job Corp facility, National Guard training area and a correctional facility for the state. During the 2003 Iraq War, Camp Atterbury was a training area for Military Police.

Above: The April 8, 1945, edition of The Indianapolis Star.

Right: Gigantic flags were used by the William H. Block Company to herald World War II victory in Europe. Soon after word of Germany's unconditional surrender was out, the 100-by-60-foot flags were unfurled from the top of the department store.

WEATHER TODAY
Fair, Little Change

THE INDIANAPOLIS STAR

FAIR AND FIRST

TELEPHONE RI. 7311
Irvington Branch IR. 0460

VOL. 43. NO. 63. ★★★ TUESDAY MORNING, AUGUST 7, 1945 FIVE CENTS.

ATOMIC BOMB MAY SPELL ANNIHILATION FOR JAPS

The Day In Indiana

By Maurice Early

Canning Waste Use
Propose Pilot Plant
Spadework Done
Need Of Economy
See Ahead To 1946

Many Hoosier Lads In Luzon Cannon Outfit

By FRANK A. WHITE
Star's Correspondent In Pacific

Top Air Ace Killed

MAJ. RICHARD BONG

Maj. Bong Dies In Test Flight Crash

Army's No. 1 Flier Killed In Trial Of P-80 Shooting Star

Billions Of Uranium Atoms Used In King Of Explosives

Earth Shaker Hits Hiroshima To Seal Surrender Demand

The Osaka radio, without referring to any possible damage from an atomic bomb dropped on Hiroshima, announced Monday the cancellation of various trains in Hiroshima prefecture and other areas.

The Japanese Domei news agency, quoted by BBC, said today that the "extent of damage" to Hiroshima was now under investigation.

By JOHN M. HIGHTOWER

Washington, Aug. 6 (AP)—The most terrible destructive force ever harnessed by man—atomic energy—is now being turned on the islands of Japan by United States bombers. The Japanese face a threat of utter desolation, and their capitulation may be greatly speeded up.

Existence of the great new weapon was announced personally by President Truman in a statement issued through the White House at 11 a.m., Eastern war time. He said the first atomic bomb, invented and perfected in the United States, had been dropped on the Japanese army base of Hiroshima 16 hours before.

That one bomb alone carried a wallop more violent than 2,000 B-29 Superfortresses normally could hand an enemy city, using old type TNT bombs.

AND BOMBS OF THIS TYPE are only a beginning. Mr. Truman said that while these are now in production "even more powerful forms are in development."

Initial reports on the dreadful power of the atomic explosive come from Los Alamos, N.M., where it was tested July 16. A steel tower holding the test model was vaporized when it went off. A great crater was torn in the earth. Windows rattled 250 miles away and forest rangers 150 miles off thought there had been an earthquake. A brilliant light flamed over the whole landscape.

Something like that is believed to have happened at Hiroshima, though in his statement the President had no results to reveal.

Secretary of War Henry L. Stimson followed through with a report that the blast stirred a cloud of smoke and dust so impenetrable as to make immediate, accurate observation of results impossible. The power of the bomb, Stimson said, is such as to "stagger the imagination" and he asserted it would "prove a tremendous aid" in shortening the Japanese war.

STIMSON'S EMPHASIS on this point renewed speculation all over again as to whether Japan may be completely crushed by air attack without invasion.

Mr. Truman noted that the Japanese rejected the surrender ultimatum from Potsdam and that this had been intended to spare the Japanese people from "utter destruction."

City's Budget Before Council

Ordinance Proposed To Control Taxicabs

Marion County Fair Opens

Exhibit Entries Hit New Mark

Servicemen On Honor Roll

Truman Tells Ship Crew Of Mighty Blow

Jap "Mystery Town" Destroyed By Bombers

Trial At Fort To Continue

Defendant Breaks; Shift To Billings

Baby Judith, Hit By Postal Truck, Battles For Life

Court To Hear Veteran's Plea

Stricken Man Seeks Home For Children

5 Soldiers Killed, 8 Hurt, In Crash

Atomic Energy In Peacetime May Run Autos, Ships, Plants

Senator Hiram W. Johnson, Dean Of Republicans, Dies

The Weather

In Today's Star

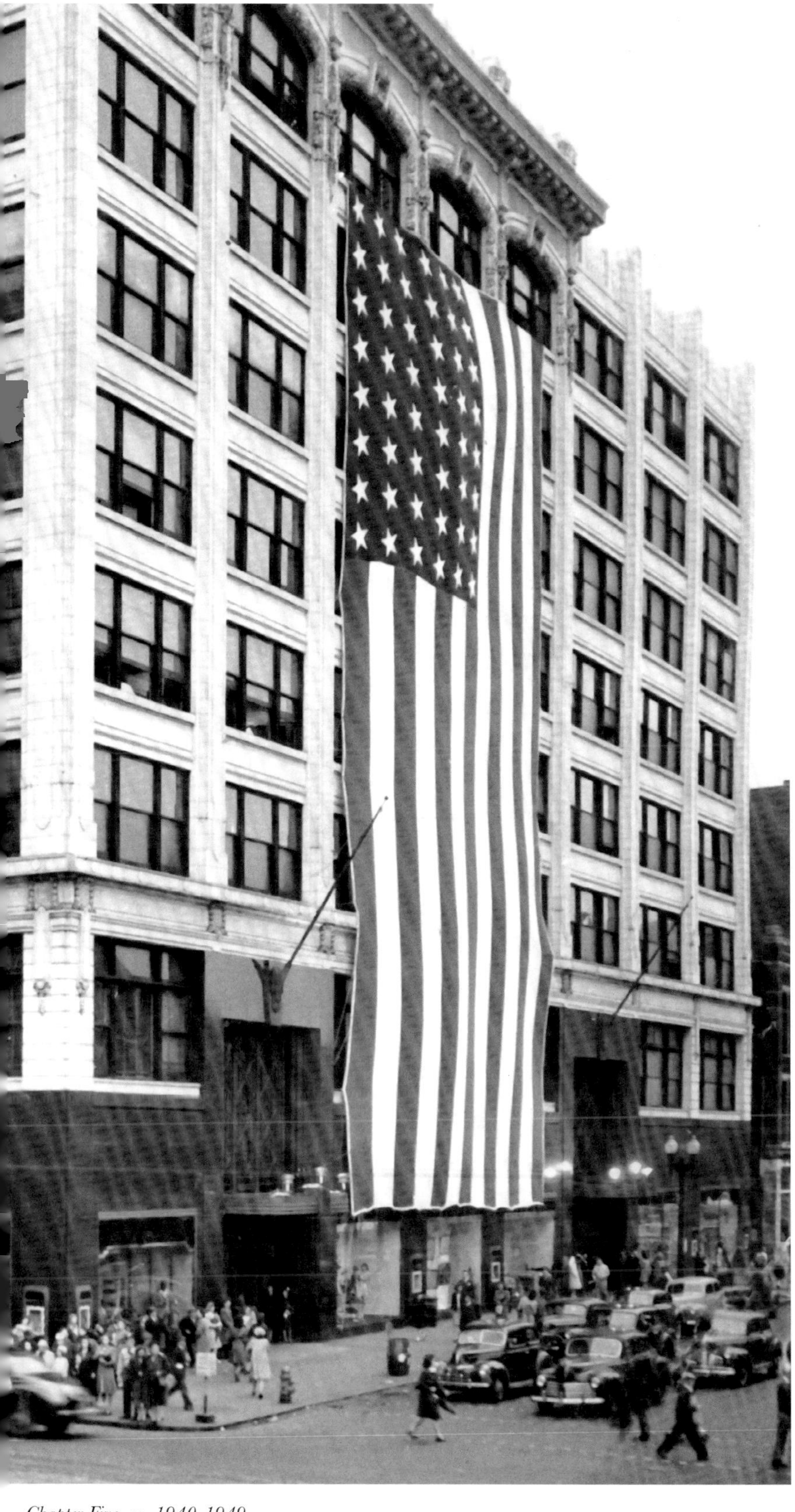

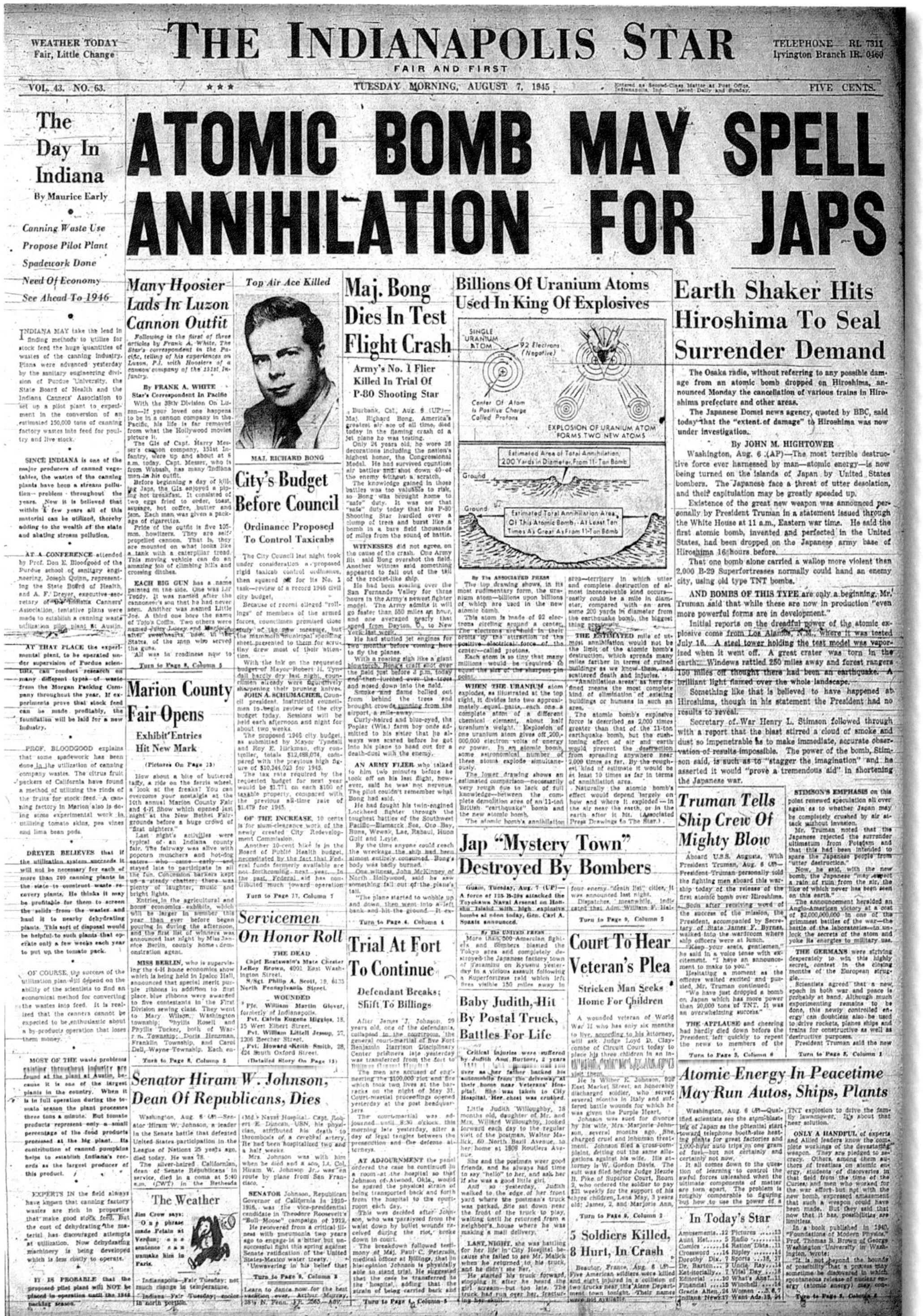

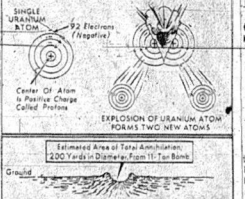

Above: The Aug. 7, 1945, edition of The Indianapolis Star.

Above: The Aug. 15, 1945, edition of The Indianapolis Star.

Right: Thousands of cheering spectators jam both sides of Meridian Street and clamber atop railings on the west side of the Federal Building to catch a glimpse of the Indianapolis Victory Parade as it moves north from Monument Circle to New York Street, August 1945.

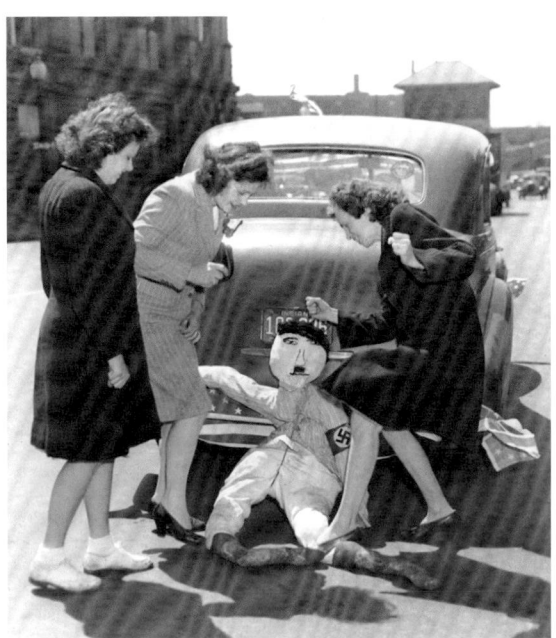

Left: When Private James Millay sent his wife a swastika armband from Europe; she fashioned the dummy of Hitler and laid it aside for V-E Day. When V-E Day came, she dragged the effigy through the downtown streets and then to the city morgue demanding its cremation. Fay DeBoor (left) and Isabelle Bunham (right) join Mrs. Millay (center).

Above: Neighborhood youngsters form their own VJ Day parade, 1945.

Above: Merchants Bank Building, Meridian and Washington streets, circa 1947.

Right: Emmett Kelly, the world's most famous circus clown and a native Hoosier entertains the audience during Ringling Brothers' and Barnum & Bailey Circus' visit to Indianapolis in 1945.

Below, left: Geist Reservoir, named after the late Clarence H. Geist, former president of the Indianapolis Water Company, circa 1946.

Below, right: Naval ordinance plant at the U.S. Naval Avionics facility, October 1946.

Above, left: The polio-paralyzed limbs of Judith Vore, 5, are limbered in this Hubbard tub by Miss Ruth Reeve, student physio-therapist at the James Whitcomb Riley Hospital for Children. August 1949.

Above, right: F. J. Brown (left), member of the flying team that delivered The Star's upstate air route, hands a bundle of papers to pilot Marvin Seagrave, June 1949.

Right: Charles Manson, 14, was back in custody in Indianapolis on Oct. 19, 1949, charged with attempted burglary after escaping from the Indiana Boys School near Plainfield. At 16, he escaped again and drove a stolen car to California. He later founded his "family" in San Francisco's Haight-Ashbury district. Manson and three female followers were sentenced to death for the Aug. 9, 1969, murders of actress Sharon Tate and six others. The sentences were reduced to life in prison in 1977.

Below: Construction of the American Legion Building at 700 N. Pennsylvania Street, May 5, 1949.

Chapter Five ~ 1940-1949

The Good Life
1950 - 1959

The 1950s hit like a bomb, releasing pent-up demands from 15 years of sacrifice, into a housing explosion that brought sidewalks and swing sets to bucolic settings across Marion County.

After a depression and a war, this decade's philosophy was: If you want it, buy it, because there is nothing stopping you from having a better life.

From the executive to the newest hire on the late shift down at the plant, owning a home became the best way to achieve the American dream. It was the good life as portrayed by Hollywood and television, populated by confident dads, perky mothers and glowing children.

It was the '50s, and TV had surpassed radio for family entertainment. Far from the futuristic gadget that was demonstrated at the Indiana State Fair in 1939, more than 137,000 sets were in Indianapolis homes by 1953.

In 1955, a housing development called Eagledale sprouted on Indianapolis' Westside near 34th Street and Georgetown Road. Depression and war had kept the home construction industry dormant for nearly two decades and now ads started appearing in the newspaper for small homes ranging in price from $10,000 to $15,000 with maintenance-free aluminum exteriors and connected by sidewalks and concrete streets. There were plenty of takers, and within four years, 10,000 people were living in Eagledale's 3,400 homes. By the end of the decade, the city had nearly 52,000 new homes.

To get to those houses, people needed cars. So, the '50s also was the decade of the car. And an expanding road system, including plans for interstate highways, made it easier for the outlying areas to flourish.

Although whites were the primary beneficiaries, black families also found a way out of neighborhoods where they had been confined for years as the civil rights movement progressed and increased job opportunities became available. The Grandview development in Washington Township became the first predominantly black neighborhood outside the city limits.

Indianapolis was still a segregated city and the major battles for civil rights would not be fought, and won, for another decade. But change was coming. In 1955, Crispus Attucks High School took center stage when it won the all-city and state basketball championships. Led by a star player, Oscar Robertson, Attucks defeated Gary Roosevelt in the first-ever state championship between two largely black schools.

"White flight" in reaction to busing wouldn't come for another decade, but the trend had already begun as more affluent white families moved to the newer neighborhoods outside of Center Township.

In the fall of 1954, The Star's business editor, Don G. Campbell, wrote of the "frightening talk" going around that the Downtown business district was slowly dying with the advent of fringe shopping areas and the mass migration to the suburbs.

One such shopping area was a new development just east of Keystone Avenue along 38th Street. The Meadows Shopping Center opened in 1956, making it one of the city's first shopping centers – boasting 2,000 parking spaces.

The center was next to the Meadowbrook Apartments, a series of 56 modern-looking low-rise buildings with plenty of green space. They had opened three years earlier and were aimed at singles and young married couples in the middle-income range.

Eastgate Shopping Center on the Eastside was completed in 1957, Glendale on the Northside opened in 1958, and Devington Plaza on the Northeastside was done in 1959.

The opening of Shadeland Avenue after World War II made it easier for factories to locate in outlying areas, too. Western Electric opened a plant along Shadeland in 1950, and Chrysler followed suit in 1952.

In 1958, 1,000 people met at the Murat Temple the week before Thanksgiving to learn that planners and consultants had devised a $500 million plan to guide the city during the next 25 years.

They envisioned a parklike area for boating and recreation along White River; installing a block-long reflecting pool complete with trees and grass as part of War Memorial Plaza; and replacing dingy buildings to the west of the Statehouse with a park, lagoon and apartments.

Opposite page: Homemakers join to sweep an unidentified street during the city's annual Clean-Up Week in April 1952.

Above: Eugene C. Pulliam, former publisher of The Star and the News, circa 1950.

Right: The Indianapolis Star's society department members in 1950 included (from left) Katherine E. Pickett, women's editor; Evelyn Imel Rhamy; Marilyn Behymer (foreground); and Barbara Fark.

Below, left: Indianapolis Star building, September 1950.

Below, right: The Star-News "Quick-Action" Want Ads telephone room, 1951. Ad takers handled an average of 2,000 calls a day, receiving and helping write the selling messages.

Above, left: Jewish children attending Hebrew School, circa 1950.

Above, right: Indianapolis children smile in spite of their poverty and hunger. They are about to receive gifts through the Christmas Cheer Fund, sponsored by The Indianapolis News. Circa November 1950.

Below: Ben Davis High School student Mary Timberman learns to drive in a car with dual controls donated to the school by Capitol Motors, Inc. Beside her is driving instructor Gordon E. Harker, who was director of athletics and safety at Ben Davis.

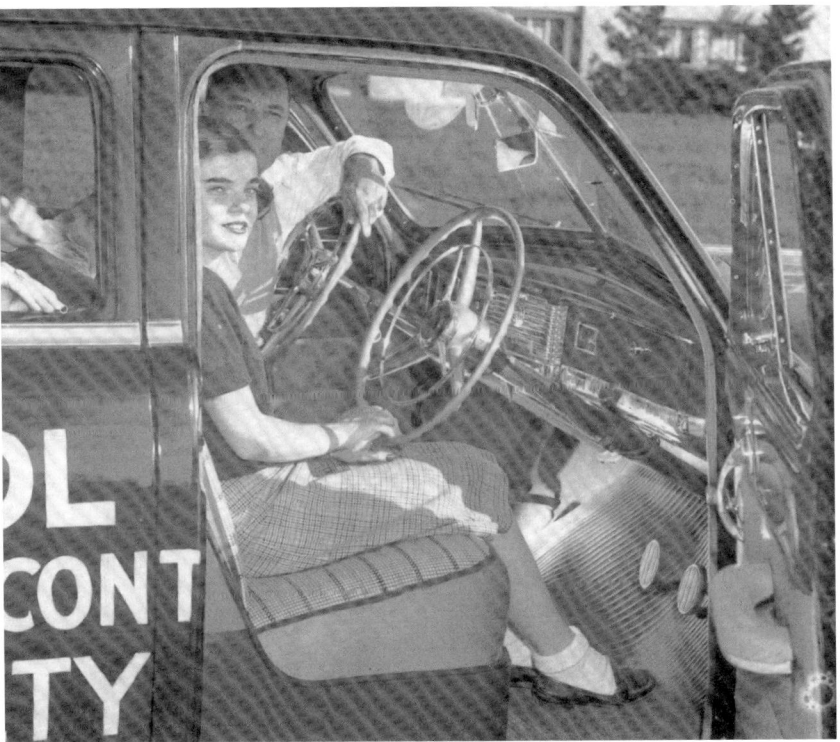

Above: The Polk Sanitary Milk Company at 1100 East 15th Street had a unique design – huge milk bottles at each corner of the entrance side. Touting its dairy products as "Polk's Best," the company was formed July 7, 1893, by James T. Polk of Greenwood. The milk plant on East 15th Street in Indianapolis, shown here Aug. 25, 1952, was built in 1910.

Above: Youngsters form victory parade for Dwight D. Eisenhower in 1952 stopping traffic in the 4700 block of East 34th Street while they paraded. Appropriately leading the march was Patty Isenhower, 9 years old, and her sister, Sue, 4. They are followed (left to right) by neighborhood youngsters Jerry Dodd, 6; Mark Dodd, 4; David Dodd, 8; Nancy Hughes, 6; Sandra Hughes, 9; and Larry Willman, 4.

Left: Indianapolis Star composing room employees use linotype machines, circa 1953.

Below: Three of a group of 150 carriers of The Indianapolis Star who won a two-day trip to Chicago in a circulation contest board a train to the Windy City, August 1953. Waving goodbye are (left to right) Bobby Woodard, Jerry Brice and Billy Lyng. The brakeman is Russell Barney.

Above: The small southern Indiana town of Milan won the Indiana High School state basketball championship by defeating powerhouse Muncie Central in a final game that was settled only when Milan's Bobby Plump hit his fabled last-second shot. The David and Goliath story was the inspiration for the movie, "Hoosiers".

Above: Detective Sergeants Spurgeon D. Davenport (left) and James W. Rogers of the Indianapolis Police Department were pictured in The Star on Jan. 6, 1953, after they were credited with following a baffling trail through Indianapolis and Chicago underworlds in order to solve two supermarket robberies.

Above, right: Star publisher Eugene C. Pulliam and his wife are shown here with children of employees during a 1954 company picnic at "The Fourth Estate," a private park for employees of The Star and The News.

Right: Rehearsing a Sunday morning inter-denominational broadcast are (left to right, front row) Sue Ellen Butler, Stanley Walker, and Mark Fletcher, and (back row) Max and David Miller, the Rev. Jim Jones and Carl Grim. Rev. Jones preached at several Indianapolis churches before founding the "Peoples Temple." See related pictures on page 99.

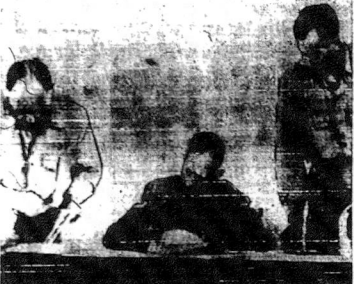

Above: The July 27, 1953, edition of The Indianapolis Star announces the end of the Korean War.

Above: Raking leaves at Public School 43, West 40th Street and North Capitol Avenue, are (left to right) Harriette Conn, Mrs. Ralph Jackson and Judy Jackson. The girls are members of a new Girl Scout troop, led by Mrs. Jackson, which chose the leaf-raking project for C-Day, 1955.

Below: Pitman-Moore Company workers Thomas Baker (left) and Chester McDermet begin loading packages of Salk polio vaccine vials into a delivery truck for delivery to Weir Cook Municipal Airport in 1955.

Above: The March 20, 1955, edition of The Indianapolis Star.

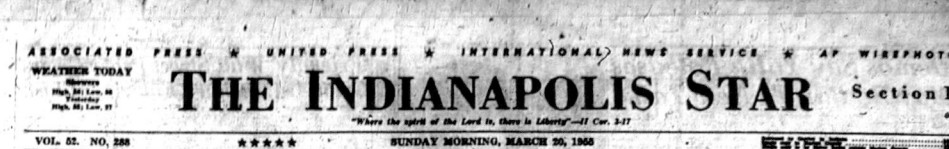

Above: Oscar Robertson and teammate William Brown accept the Indiana State High School championship trophy from J. Edgar Stahl. Robertson led his Crispus Attucks High School team to two straight Indiana state championships in 1955-56. He starred at the University of Cincinnati and was drafted by the Cincinnati Royals. Robertson was elected to Naismith Memorial Basketball Hall of Fame in 1980.

Below: Indiana State Fair visitors look over the Indianapolis Star exhibit on the second floor of the grandstand, Sept. 3, 1955. The display introduced visitors to the top editors and columnists and explained how news and pictures from throughout the world were collected for each day's edition.

Above: Boy Scout Curtis Downs is given an honorary fireman's helmet by Captain Charles Hill at Fire Station No. 1 as the first fire company-sponsored Scout troop in Indianapolis was activated there, May 1959. Also shown are Scout Paul Carter and Captain Howard Clark, scoutmaster of the new Troop No. 413.

Right: Gary Vaughn (right), 18-year old winner of the 1955 Soap Box Derby, with Bob Amos, 14, who competed in his fourth derby in July 1959. The Indianapolis Star was the local sponsor of the derby from 1934 to 1964. In 1953, the Wilbur Shaw Memorial Hill was built at 30th and Cold Spring Road. The hill was named after the three-time Indianapolis 500 winner.

Above, left: State Senator Robert L. Brokenburr during his eighth term as a Marion County senator, January 1959.

Above, right: A crowd estimated at 20,000 jams the southern half of Monument Circle to hear evangelist Billy Graham preach Oct. 29, 1959.

Left: The first African-American elected judge in Indiana, Mercer M. Mance signs his oath of office as he prepares to take the bench in Superior Court in January 1959. Michael B. Reddington, City Corporation Counsel witnesses the signing of the oath.

Tumultuous Times

1960 - 1969

This was a decade that should have come with a warning label like those found on aerosol cans: Caution, contents under pressure.

Nationally and internationally the decade was notorious as a period of tumultuous change and tragic events. It was no picnic locally either.

It started in 1960 with the horrific sight of a temporary scaffold collapsing at the Indianapolis Motor Speedway during the pace lap of the race, killing two people. It ended in 1969 with a large disturbance and mass arrests of blacks after the Fire Department was prevented from reaching a burning building on Indiana Avenue.

In between, came the city's worst disaster: A leaking propane tank exploded on Halloween night, 1963, at the Indiana State Fairgrounds Coliseum, killing 74 ice show spectators and injuring more than 400 others. And in 1965, 16-year-old Sylvia Likens was found tortured to death in one of the city's most remembered crimes.

But it was not all bleak news. It was during the 60s that the city took its first tentative steps toward revitalizing Downtown. A new City-County Building was completed in 1962 and, a few years later, the original city government building was converted for use as the Indiana State Museum.

The interstate highway system was largely completed during the 1960s, carving through established neighborhoods, but also making it possible to bring visitors Downtown more easily – which would be key to the development that followed.

Lockerbie Square became the city's first established historic district, and city and county governments approved plans to merge governments into what would be called Uni-gov.

The city also got its first zoo and Clowes Hall opened at Butler University. WTLC-FM, the first black-oriented radio station in Indianapolis, went on the air in 1968.

On the circle, the Soldiers and Sailors Monument was decorated with holiday lights and transformed into "the world's largest Christmas Tree" for the first time in 1962.

The Indiana Pacers played their first game in 1967 and the following year Indianapolis had its first enclosed shopping mall when Lafayette Square opened.

But despite these positive developments, the 1960s were overshadowed by frightening headlines of war, civil unrest and assassinations.

In 1968, when word came that Martin Luther King Jr. had been assasinated in Memphis, another national leader happened to be in Indianapolis. Senator Robert F. Kennedy was seeking the Democratic nomination for president and was on his way to a campaign stop in Indianapolis when he was told of King's death.

And so it was Kennedy who broke the news of King's death to a mostly black crowd of about 2,500 supporters who had gathered in the drizzling rain to hear him speak.

"I have bad news for you, for all of our fellow citizens, and people who love peace all over the world," Kennedy told the crowd, "and that is that Martin Luther King was shot and killed tonight." A gasp was heard in the audience and cries of "No! No!" But not everyone heard the announcement. Eventually, Kennedy's subdued demeanor captured the crowd's attention.

"For those of you who are black and are tempted to be filled with hatred and distrust at the injustice of such an act, against all white people, I can only say that I feel in my own heart the same kind of feeling. I had a member of my family killed, but he was killed by a white man."

Although there were riots in more than 100 cities across America that night, Indianapolis remained calm, and people who were there that night say Kennedy made the difference. Two months later, he was dead too.

Richard Lugar, who went on to be Indiana's longest-serving U.S. senator, was mayor of Indianapolis in the late 1960s, having served on the school board before that.

The last year of the decade provided a final flash point. One June night, a disturbance erupted on Indiana Avenue and Lugar was called back to city hall. When he learned firefighters were blockaded from a fire at a food market, he ordered police to start making arrests.

Several police officers were injured during disturbances, which spilled over into other areas. However, the city never experienced the turmoil that other cities, like Detroit and Washington, suffered.

As the decade wound down, city officials set about implementing a new government system called Uni-Gov, which merged most city and county government functions. On the west side of Downtown a new university campus was being formed from the merger of two branches, resulting in the cumbersome name, "Indiana University-Purdue University at Indianapolis," or just "IUPUI."

Opposite page: A young boy, battered by the force of the explosion, is lifted alive from the rubble of a Coliseum stand where he was trapped for nearly two hours, Oct. 31, 1963. More details on page 80.

Tragedy struck during the pace lap of the 1960 Indianapolis 500-Mile Race. A privately owned makeshift scaffold collapsed, killing two people and injuring 40. About 125 people, who had paid $5 to $10 for vantage spots on the scaffold, tumbled to the ground. Upon hearing screams behind him, Indianapolis News photographer, J. Parke Randall turned away from the track to see – and shoot – the wood-and-metal tower tumbling to the ground under the weight of jostling spectators, spewing them out onto the infield turf.

Left: Vice president Richard Nixon waves to a tumultuous crowd that showered him and his wife, Pat, with confetti as they rode in a convertible on their way to Monument Circle, September 1960.

Below, left: Vice president Nixon speaks on The Circle, September 1960.

Below: In the 1960s, Riverside Park was in decline financially, and it also came under fire for its segregationist policies. Black children were only permitted at the park during designated "Colored Frolic Days." Protests against the park brought an end to the restriction, but the park's financial troubles were another matter and it was closed in 1970.

Chapter Seven ~ 1960-1969

75

Left: U.S. Sen. John F. Kennedy at his campaign headquarters on North Meridian Street, March 21, 1960.

Below: Senator Kennedy addresses a capacity crowd of 11,000 at the Fairgrounds Coliseum Oct. 10, 1960. Roughly 2,000 people sitting at tables on the main floor of the arena paid $100 a plate to hear the Democratic presidential candidate speak. Sitting in the right foreground is Democratic gubernatorial candidate, Senator Matthew Welsh.

Right: Civil rights demonstration in front of Woolworth Store, March 1960.

Above: Patrons fill Clowes Hall, on the Butler University campus, for the opening night concert on Oct. 18, 1963.

Above: After holiday lights were strung from the 284-foot Soldiers and Sailors Monument in 1962, it became known as the "world's tallest Christmas tree." That claim, not entirely accurate in the first place, was usurped 20 years later by the King's Island amusement park in Ohio, which hung lights from its 330-foot Eiffel Tower replica.

Left: Nine year-old Terry Thimlar couldn't participate in this 1963 Indianapolis Indians baseball clinic at old Victory Field, but after surgery to repair his polio-damaged left leg he went on to play sports at Pike High school, where his basketball team won sectional and regional titles during his senior year in 1972.

Above: A peaceful parade of 2,000 marched through the streets of Indianapolis to an NAACP rally held at University Park on Aug. 4, 1963. The rally called for advances for blacks in employment, housing, education, politics and public housing.

Above: Construction of Indiana Bell building, 1963. *Courtesy Bass Photo Collection, (311877-F), Indiana Historical Society*

Above: Aerial view of Indianapolis including Monument Circle, circa 1962. *Courtesy Bass Photo Collection, (309612), Indiana Historical Society*

Left: Loew's Theatre, circa 1963. Opened in 1921 as Loews State at 35 North Pennsylvania Street and renamed Loews Palace in 1928. The building was demolished in 1970. *Courtesy Bass Photo Collection, (310572 2), Indiana Historical Society*

Right: Keith's Theater in the 1960s. Opened as the Grand Opera House at 117 N. Pennsylvania in 1875. Renamed B.F. Keith's Theatre in 1910. The theater closed in 1964. *Courtesy Bass Photo Collection, (3313830), Indiana Historical Society*

O ct. 31, 1963, will forever be remembered in Indianapolis as the night an explosion ripped through the Indiana State Fairgrounds Coliseum, claiming the lives of 74 people and injuring nearly 400. It was one of the worst tragedies in Indiana history.

It was opening night for the Holiday on Ice show, with more than 4,000 spectators on hand. Propane, being used to keep pre-popped popcorn warm, was leaking from a faulty valve. At 11:04 p.m. an explosion sent bodies flying nearly 60 feet. A second blast took place a few minutes later, caused by heat rising and air rushing into the vacuumized area. Most victims were either severely burned or crushed by concrete.

Indianapolis was not equipped to handle the volume of dead. Coroner Dennis Nicholas elected to use the Coliseum as a makeshift morgue. The bodies were placed on plywood and lined up on the ice according to gender and age. Family members passed through the rows of bodies to identify their loved ones.

Sixty five people were killed that evening and eight others would die in the days and weeks that followed. The 74th victim died Feb. 7, 1964.

In 2002, the Indiana State Fair Commission dedicated a plaque memorializing the tragedy.

The Coliseum was restored and continued to be used for many events. It was renamed the Pepsi Coliseum in 1991.

Above: The Nov. 2, 1963, edition of The Indianapolis Star.

Above, left: Firefighters dig through the rubble in a frantic search for survivors.

Above, right: Deputy Coroner Leighton George waits in a room at the Coliseum for relatives of victims of the explosion to claim personal effects.

Left: A crane removes wreckage after an explosion during an ice show at the State Fairgrounds Coliseum on Oct. 31, 1963. The blast, which killed 74, was touched off by gas leaking from a propane tank near a popcorn warmer. The ice became a temporary morgue for the blanket-covered bodies.

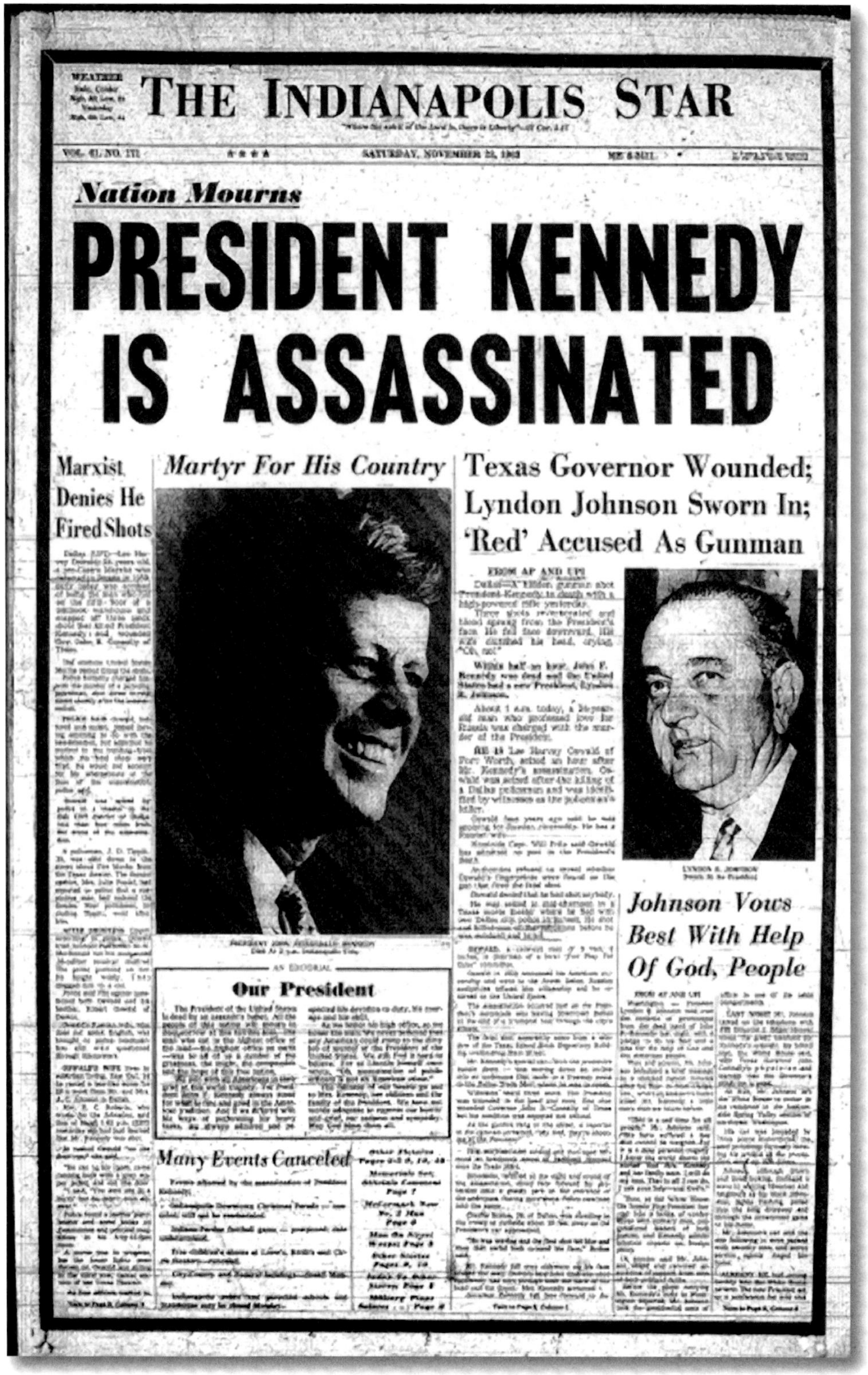

THE INDIANAPOLIS STAR

SATURDAY, NOVEMBER 23, 1963

Nation Mourns

PRESIDENT KENNEDY IS ASSASSINATED

Marxist Denies He Fired Shots

Martyr For His Country

Texas Governor Wounded; Lyndon Johnson Sworn In; 'Red' Accused As Gunman

FROM AP AND UPI

Johnson Vows Best With Help Of God, People

AN EDITORIAL

Our President

Many Events Canceled

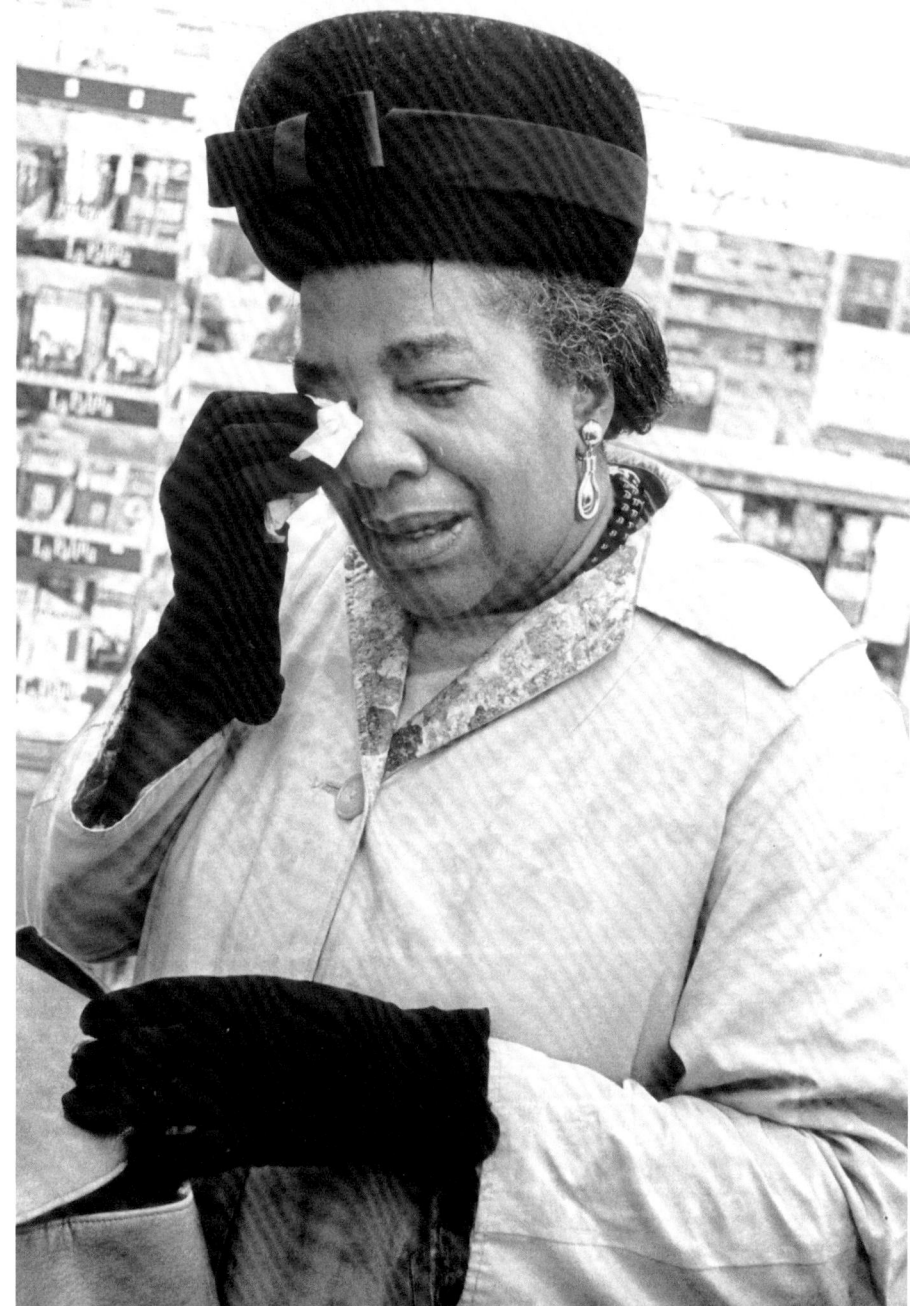

Above: The Nov. 23, 1963, edition of The Indianapolis Star.

Above: Indianapolis resident Mrs. Frances Cunningham reacts to the news that President John F. Kennedy had been killed.

Left: After nearly 20 years of planning, the Indianapolis Zoo opened on April 18, 1964, in Washington Park, on the city's northeast side. In the early 1980s, the city decided the zoo had outgrown it's 24 acres and decided to move the zoo to the White River State Park.

Below: Checking out the train at the new zoo, August 1964. Gordon E. Harker engineers for (left to right) Debbie Whyte, 7 years old; Jimmy Whyte, 3; Holly Kappes, 2; George Tiniera, 3; Kirby Whyte, 9, and Jeff MacLennan, 5.

Above: Police arrest three men involved in a 1964 Congress of Racial Equality (CORE) sit-in at the old Indianapolis School Board building, 150 N. Meridian Street. The men, (front to back) John Torian, Alfonzo Black and James Pond, demanded the integration of teaching staffs in Indianapolis schools. CORE supporters carrying signs reading "Why a Black Attucks?" and "Integrate Attucks Staff" also picketed construction of an addition to Attucks High School. That night, the Indianapolis Board of Education rejected a plea by CORE that all school construction be stopped until "de facto" segregation was eliminated. Attucks' teaching staff was integrated in the late 1960s, but segregation of students continued into the 1970s, despite the state's 1949 desegregation law.

Above: Pickets of the Congress of Racial Equality march in front of Crispus Attucks High School in 1964 while construction of a new addition continues.

Left: Parnelli Jones jumps from his car, which caught fire while entering the pits during the 1964 Indianapolis 500.

Right: The Beatles arrive for two Indianapolis concerts in 1964. *State Archives, Indiana Commission on Public Records*

Above: The Beatles performing at the Coliseum in 1964. *Photo courtesy Indiana State Fair*

On the evening of Palm Sunday, April 11, 1965, three twisters swept through the state, all north of Indianapolis. Some of the worst damage was in Howard County. The storm flattened Alto, decimated Greentown and obliterated the downtown of Russiaville. The tornados killed more than 140 people and injured nearly 2,000. It was the worst tornado disaster in Indiana history and prompted the state to develop comprehensive tornado planning.

Left: Aftermath of the tornado that roared through a small suburb near Marion, 1965.

Above: Surviving residents of a mobile home park in Marion search for belongings in the wreckage after a tornado cut through the three-acre trailer park in 1965.

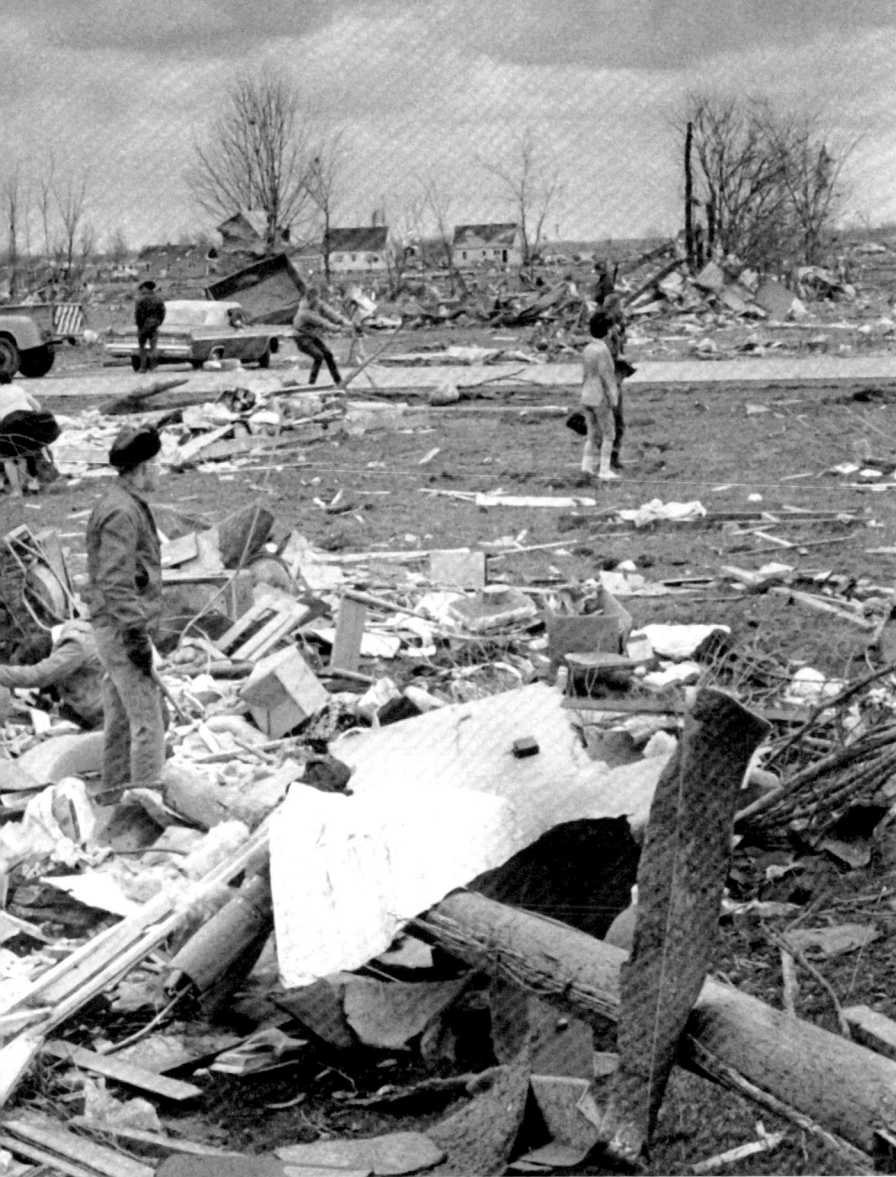

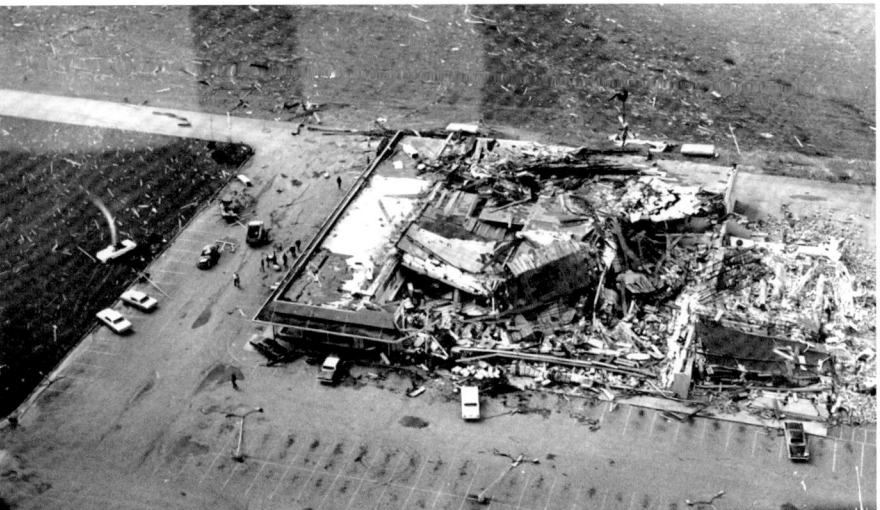

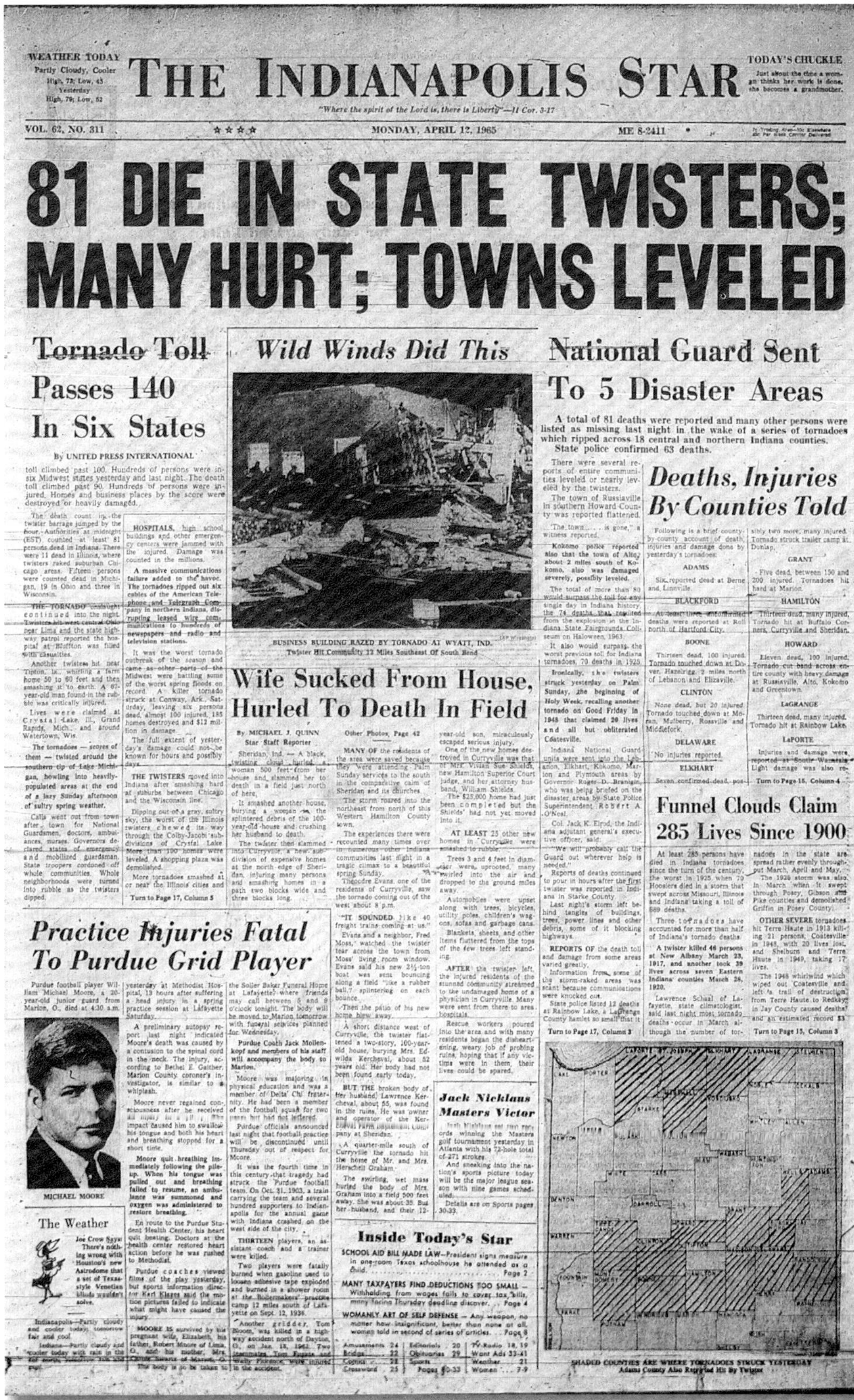

WEATHER TODAY
Partly Cloudy, Cooler
High, 73; Low, 45
Yesterday
High, 79; Low, 52

THE INDIANAPOLIS STAR

"Where the spirit of the Lord is, there is Liberty"—II Cor. 3-17

TODAY'S CHUCKLE
Just about the time a woman thinks her work is done, she becomes a grandmother.

VOL. 62, NO. 311 ★★★★ MONDAY, APRIL 12, 1965 ME 8-2411

81 DIE IN STATE TWISTERS; MANY HURT; TOWNS LEVELED

Tornado Toll Passes 140 In Six States

By UNITED PRESS INTERNATIONAL

toll climbed past 100. Hundreds of persons were in six Midwest states yesterday and last night. The death toll climbed past 90. Hundreds of persons were injured. Homes and business places by the score were destroyed or heavily damaged.

The death count in the twister barrage jumped by the hour. Authorities at midnight (EST) counted at least 81 persons dead in Indiana. There were 11 dead in Illinois, where twisters raked suburban Chicago areas. Fifteen persons were counted dead in Michigan, 19 in Ohio and three in Wisconsin.

THE TORNADO onslaught continued into the night. Twisters hit west central Ohio near Lima and the state highway patrol reported the hospital at Bluffton was filled with casualties.

Another twister hit near Tipton, Ia., whirling a farm home 50 to 60 feet and then smashing it to earth. A 67-year-old man found in the rubble was critically injured.

Lives were claimed at Crystal Lake, Ill., Grand Rapids, Mich., and around Watertown, Wis.

The tornadoes — scores of them — twisted around the southern tip of Lake Michigan, howling into heavily-populated areas at the end of a lazy Sunday afternoon of sultry spring weather.

Calls went out from town after town for National Guardsmen, doctors, ambulances, nurses. Governors declared states of emergency and mobilized guardsman. State troopers cordoned off whole communities. Whole neighborhoods were turned into rubble as the twisters dipped.

HOSPITALS, high school buildings and other emergency centers were jammed with the injured. Damage was counted in the millions.

A massive communications failure added to the havoc. The tornadoes ripped out six cables of the American Telephone and Telegraph Company in northern Indiana, disrupting leased wire communications to hundreds of newspapers and radio and television stations.

It was the worst tornado outbreak of the season and came as other parts of the Midwest were battling some of the worst spring floods on record. A killer tornado struck at Conway, Ark., Saturday, leaving six persons dead, almost 100 injured, 185 homes destroyed and $12 million in damage.

The full extent of yesterday's damage could not be known for hours and possibly days.

THE TWISTERS moved into Indiana after smashing hard at suburbs between Chicago and the Wisconsin line.

Dipping out of a gray, sultry sky, the worst of the Illinois twisters chewed its way through the Colby-Jacobi subdivisions of Crystal Lake. More than 100 homes were leveled. A shopping plaza was demolished.

More tornadoes smashed at or near the Illinois cities and

Turn to Page 17, Column 5

Wild Winds Did This

BUSINESS BUILDING RAZED BY TORNADO AT WYATT, IND.
Twister Hit Community 12 Miles Southeast Of South Bend

Wife Sucked From House, Hurled To Death In Field

By MICHAEL J. QUINN
Star Staff Reporter

Other Photos, Page 42

Sheridan, Ind. — A black, twisting cloud hurled a woman 500 feet from her house and slammed her to death in a field just north of here.

It smashed another house, burying a woman in the splintered debris of the 100-year-old house and crushing her husband to death.

The twister then slammed into Curryville, a new subdivision of expensive homes at the north edge of Sheridan, injuring many persons and smashing homes in a path two blocks wide and three blocks long.

MANY OF the residents of the area were saved because they were attending Palm Sunday services to the south in the comparative calm of Sheridan and its churches.

The storm roared into the northeast from north of this Western Hamilton County town.

The experiences there were recounted many times over in numerous other Indiana communities last night in a tragic climax to a beautiful spring Sunday.

Theodore Evans, one of the residents of Curryville, saw the tornado coming out of the west about 8 p.m.

"IT SOUNDED like 40 freight trains coming at us."

Evans and a neighbor, Fred Moss, watched the twister tear across the town from Moss' living room window. Evans said his new 2½-ton boat was sent bouncing along a field "like a rubber ball," splintering on each bounce.

Then the patio of his new home blew away.

A short distance west of Curryville, the twister flattened a two-story, 100-year-old house, burying Mrs. Edwilda Kercheval, about 82 years old. Her body had not been found early today.

BUT THE broken body of her husband, Lawrence Kercheval, about 55, was found in the ruins. He was owner and operator of the Kercheval Farm Implement Company at Sheridan.

A quarter-mile south of Curryville the tornado hit the home of Mr. and Mrs. Herschell Graham.

The swirling, wet mass hurled the body of Mrs. Graham into a field 500 feet away. She was about 35. But her husband, and their 12-year-old son, miraculously escaped serious injury.

One of the new homes destroyed in Curryville was that of Mrs. Vivian Sue Shields, new Hamilton Superior Court judge, and her attorney husband, William Shields.

The $25,000 home had just been completed but the Shields' had not yet moved into it.

AT LEAST 25 other new homes in Curryville were smashed to rubble.

Trees 3 and 4 feet in diameter were uprooted, many swirled into the air and dropped to the ground miles away.

Automobiles were upset along with trees, bicycles, utility poles, children's wagons, sofas and garbage cans.

Blankets, sheets, and other items fluttered from the tops of the few trees left standing.

AFTER the twister left, the injured residents of the stunned community streamed to the undamaged home of a physician in Curryville. Many were sent from there to area hospitals.

Rescue workers poured into the area and with many residents began the disheartening, weary job of probing ruins, hoping that if any victims were in them, their lives could be spared.

National Guard Sent To 5 Disaster Areas

A total of 81 deaths were reported and many other persons were listed as missing last night in the wake of a series of tornadoes which ripped across 18 central and northern Indiana counties. State police confirmed 63 deaths.

There were several reports of entire communities leveled or nearly leveled by the twisters.

The town of Russiaville in southern Howard County was reported flattened.

"The town . . . is gone," a witness reported.

Kokomo police reported also that the town of Alto, about 2 miles south of Kokomo, also was damaged severely, possibly leveled.

The total of more than 80 would surpass the toll for any single day in Indiana history, the 74 deaths that resulted from the explosion in the Indiana State Fairgrounds Coliseum on Haloween, 1963.

It also would surpass the worst previous toll for Indiana tornadoes, 70 deaths in 1925.

Ironically, the twisters struck yesterday on Palm Sunday, the beginning of Holy Week, recalling another tornado on Good Friday in 1948 that claimed 20 lives and all but obliterated Coatesville.

Indiana National Guard units were sent into the Lebanon, Elkhart, Kokomo, Marion and Plymouth areas by Governor Roger D. Branigin, who was being briefed on the disaster areas by State Police Superintendent Robert A. O'Neal.

Col. Jack K. Elrod, the Indiana adjutant general's executive officer, said:

"We will probably call the Guard out wherever help is needed."

Reports of deaths continued to pour in hours after the first twister was reported in Indiana in Starke County.

Last night's storm left behind tangles of buildings, trees, power lines and other debris, some of it blocking highways.

REPORTS OF the death toll and damage from some areas varied greatly.

Information from some of the storm-raked areas was scant because communications were knocked out.

State police listed 12 deaths at Rainbow Lake, a LaGrange County hamlet so small that it

Turn to Page 17, Column 3

Deaths, Injuries By Counties Told

Following is a brief county-by-county account of death, injuries and damage done by yesterday's tornadoes:

ADAMS

Six reported dead at Berne and Linnville.

BLACKFORD

At least three unconfirmed deaths were reported at Roll north of Hartford City.

BOONE

Thirteen dead, 100 injured. Tornado touched down at Dover, Hazelrigg, 2 miles north of Lebanon and Elizaville.

CLINTON

None dead, but 20 injured. Tornado touched down at Moran, Mulberry, Rossville and Middlefork.

DELAWARE

No injuries reported.

ELKHART

Seven confirmed dead, possibly two more, many injured. Tornado struck trailer camp at Dunlap.

GRANT

Five dead, between 150 and 200 injured. Tornadoes hit hard at Marion.

HAMILTON

Thirteen dead, many injured. Tornado hit at Buffalo Corners, Curryville and Sheridan.

HOWARD

Eleven dead, 100 injured. Tornado cut band across entire county with heavy damage at Russiaville, Alto, Kokomo and Greentown.

LaGRANGE

Thirteen dead, many injured. Tornado hit at Rainbow Lake.

LaPORTE

Injuries and damage were reported at South Wanatah. Light damage was also re-

Turn to Page 15, Column 4

Funnel Clouds Claim 285 Lives Since 1900

At least 285 persons have died in Indiana tornadoes since the turn of the century, the worst in 1925 when 70 Hoosiers died in a storm that swept across Missouri, Illinois and Indiana taking a toll of 689 deaths.

Three tornadoes have accounted for more than half of Indiana's tornado deaths.

A twister killed 46 persons at New Albany March 23, 1917, and another took 39 lives across seven Eastern Indiana counties March 28, 1920.

Lawrence Schaal of Lafayette, state climatologist, said last night most tornado deaths occur in March although the number of tornadoes in the state are spread rather evenly throughout March, April and May.

The 1925 storm was also in March when it swept through Posey, Gibson and Pike counties and demolished Griffin in Posey County.

OTHER SEVERE tornadoes hit Terre Haute in 1913 killing 21 persons, Coatesville in 1948, with 20 lives lost, and Shelburn and Terre Haute in 1949, taking 17 lives.

The 1948 whirlwind which wiped out Coatesville and left a trail of destruction from Terre Haute to Redkey in Jay County caused deaths and an estimated record $3

Turn to Page 15, Column 3

Practice Injuries Fatal To Purdue Grid Player

Purdue football player William Michael Moore, a 20-year-old junior guard from Marion, O., died at 4:30 a.m. yesterday at Methodist Hospital, 13 hours after suffering a head injury in a spring practice session at Lafayette Saturday.

MICHAEL MOORE

A preliminary autopsy report last night indicated Moore's death was caused by a contusion to the spinal cord in the neck. The injury, according to Bethel E. Gaither, Marion County coroner's investigator, is similar to a whiplash.

Moore never regained consciousness after he received an injury in a pile-up. The impact caused him to swallow his tongue and both his heart and breathing stopped for a short time.

Moore quit breathing immediately following the pile-up. When his tongue was pulled out and breathing failed to resume, an ambulance was summoned and oxygen was administered to restore breathing.

En route to the Purdue Student Health Center, his heart quit beating. Doctors at the health center restored heart action before he was rushed to Methodist.

Purdue coaches viewed films of the play yesterday, but sports information director Karl Klages said the motion pictures failed to indicate what might have caused the injury.

MOORE IS survived by his pregnant wife, Elizabeth, his father, Robert Moore of Lima, O., and his mother, Mrs. Clyde Swartz of Marion, O.

The body is to be taken to the Soller Baker Funeral Home at Lafayette where friends may call between 5 and 9 o'clock tonight. The body will be moved to Marion tomorrow with funeral services planned for Wednesday.

Purdue Coach Jack Mollenkopf and members of his staff will accompany the body to Marion.

Moore was majoring in physical education and was a member of Delta Chi fraternity. He had been a member of the football squad for two years but had not lettered.

Purdue officials announced last night that football practice will be discontinued until Thursday out of respect for Moore.

It was the fourth time in this century that tragedy had struck the Purdue football team. On Oct. 31, 1903, a train carrying the team and several hundred supporters to Indianapolis for the annual game with Indiana crashed on the west side of the city.

THIRTEEN players, an assistant coach and a trainer were killed.

Two players were fatally burned when gasoline used to loosen adhesive tape exploded and burned in a shower room at the Boilermakers' practice camp 12 miles south of Lafayette on Sept. 12, 1936.

Another gridder, Tom Bloom, was killed in a highway accident north of Dayton, O., on Jan. 18, 1962. Two teammates, Tom Fugate and Wally Florence, were injured in the accident.

The Weather

Joe Crow Says: There's nothing wrong with Houston's new Astrodome that a set of Texas-style Venetian blinds wouldn't solve.

Indianapolis—Partly cloudy and cooler today; tomorrow fair and cool.

Indiana—Partly cloudy and cooler today with rain in the far south; tomorrow fair and cool.

Jack Nicklaus Masters Victor

Jack Nicklaus set two records winning the Masters golf tournament yesterday in Atlanta with his 72-hole total of 271 strokes.

And sneaking into the nation's sports picture today will be the major league season with nine games scheduled.

Details are on Sports pages 30-33.

Inside Today's Star

SCHOOL AID BILL MADE LAW—President signs measure in one-room Texas schoolhouse he attended as a child. . . . Page 2

MANY TAXPAYERS FIND DEDUCTIONS TOO SMALL—Withholding from wages fails to cover tax bills, many facing Thursday deadline discover. . . Page 4

WOMANLY ART OF SELF DEFENSE—Any weapon, no matter how insignificant, better than none at all, woman told in second of series of articles. . . Page 8

Amusements	24	Editorials	20	TV-Radio	18, 19
Bridge	22	Obituaries	29	Want Ads	33-41
Comics	28	Sports		Weather	21
Crossword	25	Pages	30-33	Women	7-9

SHADED COUNTIES ARE WHERE TORNADOES STRUCK YESTERDAY

Above: The April 17, 1963, edition of The Indianapolis Star.

Left: Panorama Shopping Center in Marion after the 1965 tornado.

Left: Rabbi Soloman Silberberg carries a sacred Torah scroll to the United Orthodox Hebrew Congregation at 5879 Central Avenue as part of the formal opening of the new synagogue and the closing of Sharah Tefilla Congregation at 601 South Meridian Street, which was merged in the new congregation, February 1966.

Right: Students and Indiana University faculty members demonstrate against the United State's Vietnam policy in 1967.

Below, left: Roger 'The Rajah' Brown, helped the Indiana Pacers earn three American Basketball Association titles in the early 70s. Brown died in 1997.

Below, right: Outside The Indianapolis Star and News building, a new brilliance illuminates the alley running between and parallel to Pennsylvania and Delaware streets. The brightness is part of the building modernization program in 1968.

Above: The April 5, 1968, edition of The Indianapolis Star.

Left: Robert F. Kennedy, looking pale and shaken at the news of Martin Luther King's assassination earlier in the day, set aside his prepared speech and spoke briefly to a predominantly black crowd of 2,500 at Broadway Park located at 17th Street and Broadway on April 4, 1968. Kennedy's presence and words of comfort were credited with sparing Indianapolis the riots that plagued other cities that night.

Chapter Seven ~ 1960-1969

Above: Fort Benjamin Harrison soldiers help package 300,000 gift items for American servicemen in Vietnam after civilian volunteers failed to report for the jobs, December 1968. Packing the first shipment of gifts are (left to right) 1st Lieutenant T. C. Harvey, Sergeant James Powell, PFC Jerry Carlson and PFC Doyle Garner.

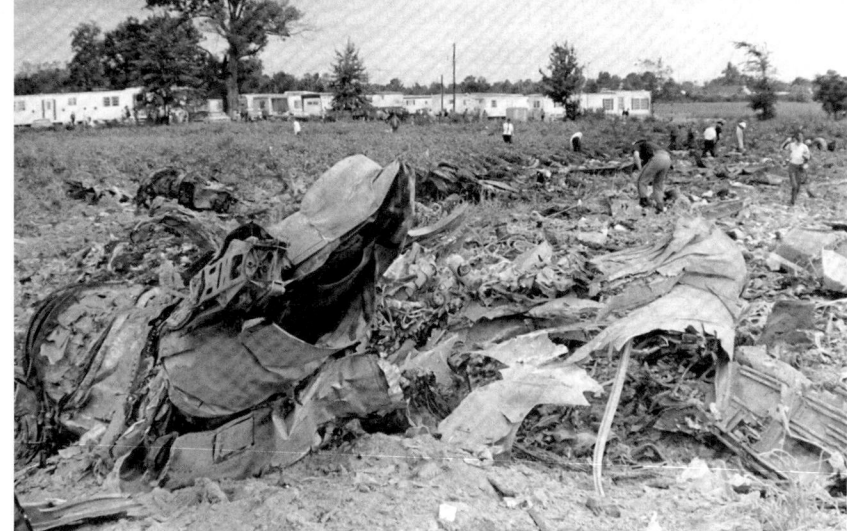

Above: The scene of the crash of an Allegheny Airlines DC9 jetliner after the Indianapolis-bound plane collided near London in Shelby County with a small private airplane, September 1969. Eighty-three persons died in the collision.

Below: Mass of wreckage covers the site of the 1969 plane crash. More than 200 trailer court residents (left) narrowly escaped the impact.

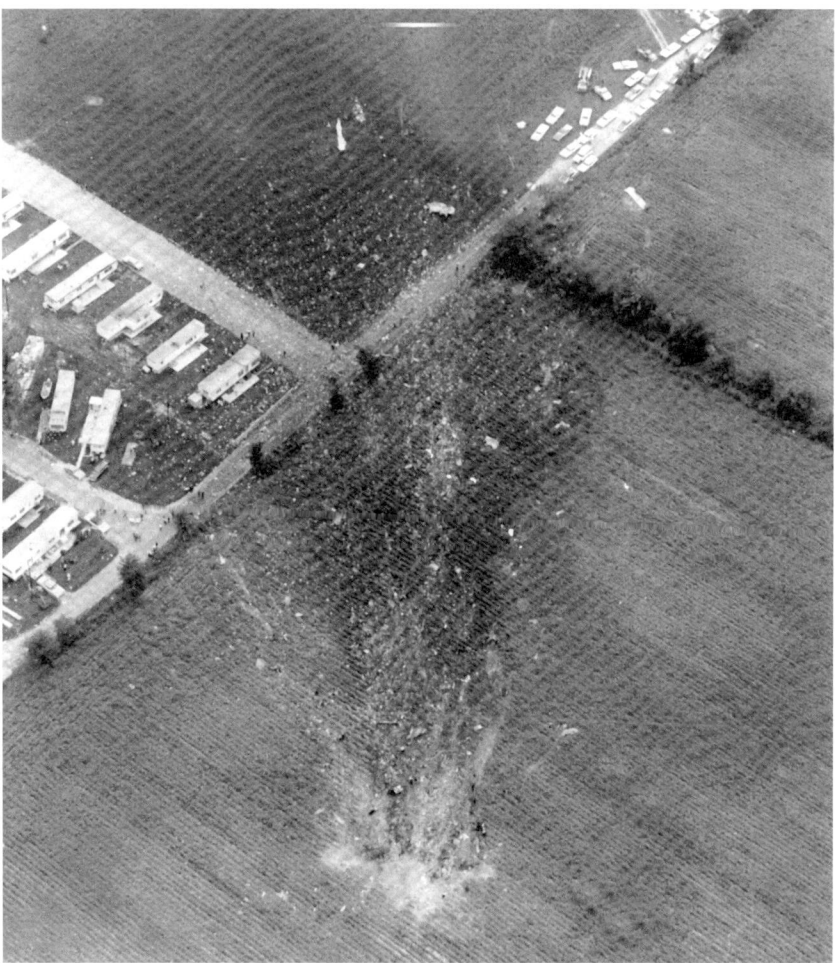

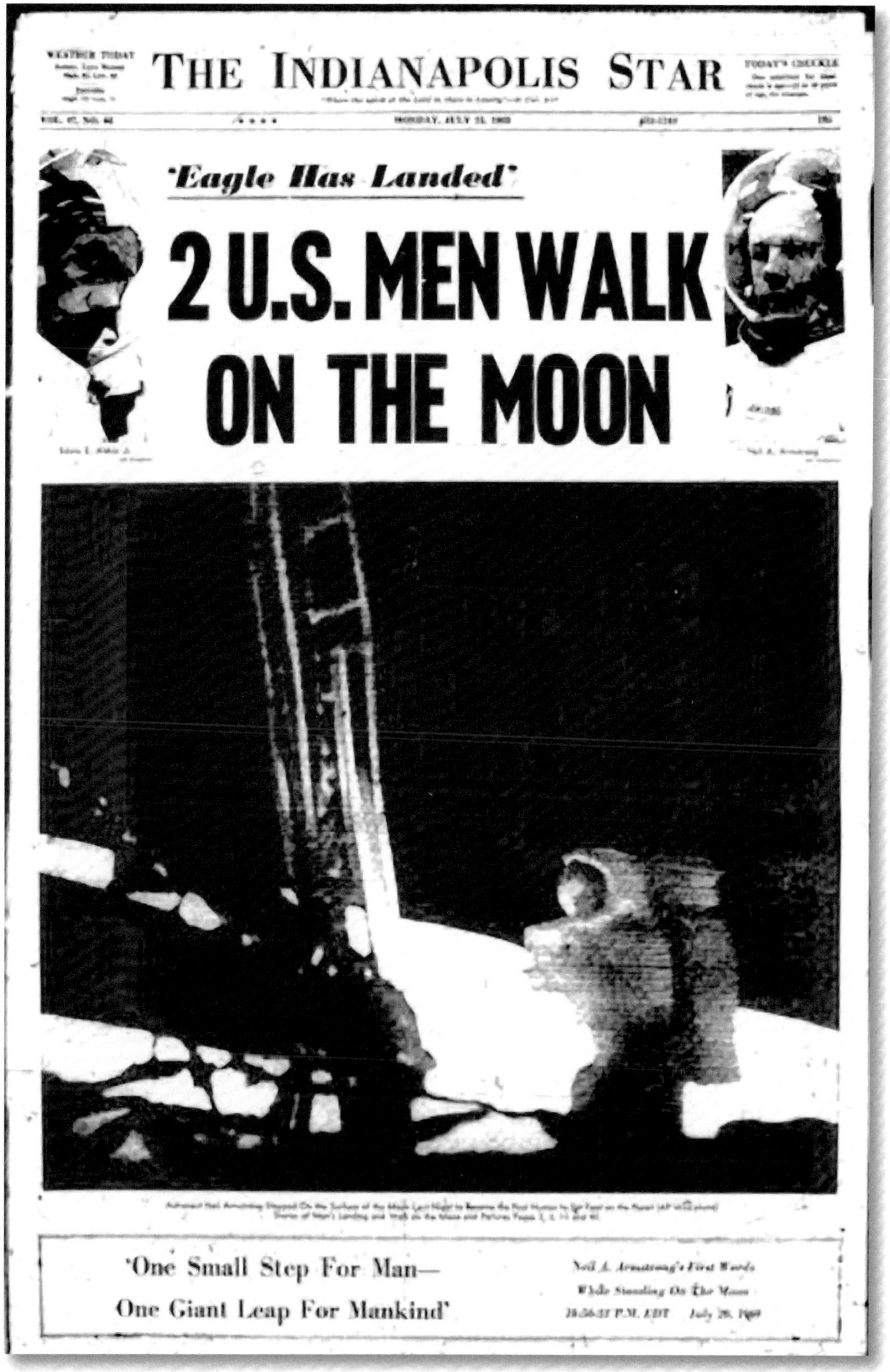

THE INDIANAPOLIS STAR

'Eagle Has Landed'

2 U.S. MEN WALK ON THE MOON

'One Small Step For Man—
One Giant Leap For Mankind'

Neil A. Armstrong's First Words
While Standing On The Moon

Above: The July 21, 1969, edition of The Indianapolis Star.

Turning Point
1970 - 1979

Downtown planners had several successes in the 1970s, but it still seemed they were struggling against the natural trend of economic development – which was outside the city center.

The Hilton Hotel (later the Radisson) became the first major hotel built Downtown since the 1920s. The Indiana National Bank tower opened in 1970; the IUPUI campus was well under way and a few years later there was the Minton-Capehart federal building.

But the real action seemed to be moving elsewhere. Inspired by the success of Lafayette Square Mall, the city's first enclosed mall which opened in 1968, Castleton Square Mall opened in 1972. Then, in quick succession, Keystone at the Crossing debuted in 1973, and Washington Square Mall opened in 1974. It was clear that the natural trend in development did not include the city center.

If Downtown seemed anemic, the energy being invested into it was not. Mayor Richard Lugar pushed ahead with the implementation of Uni-Gov, the merger of city and county government functions, which he felt would make it easier for government to lead development. It became an era of proactive government, pushing projects like the Indiana Convention Center and saving the Indiana Theatre from the wrecking ball. City planners were sometimes seen as unrealistic dreamers of big ideas, like developing the water company's Downtown canal – or perhaps even building a Downtown shopping mall. There were plenty of skeptics, and some of the ideas did sound far-fetched at the time.

When the Indiana Pacers needed a new arena, it made sense to build it in the suburbs, which was the trend in other cities. But Lugar wanted it Downtown. Market Square Arena opened in 1974, and became a Downtown concert venue as well as the home of the Pacers. In 1977, MSA was the site of Elvis Presley's last concert.

From 1967 to 1976, the Pacers were part of the American Basketball Association, winning three ABA championships in 1970, '72 and '73, all of them played at the Fairgrounds Coliseum. Then the ABA folded and the Pacers were absorbed into the National Basketball Association. But the transition was costly and the team faced a financial crisis. In 1977, a local television station conducted a telethon to sell season tickets, and the funds were raised to keep the team in Indianapolis.

Community involvement was also the basis for success for Indiana Black Expo, which started in 1971 and became an annual summertime event.

In 1974, The Indianapolis Star published a series of investigative stories about local police corruption. The Star's investigative team won the Pulitzer Prize for the series the following year.

On Feb. 8, 1977, Tony Kiritsis thrust himself forever into local crime lore when he wired a sawed-off shotgun to the neck of mortgage company executive Richard Hall and led him outside, surrounded by police and media. Upset over how he felt he had been treated by the mortgage company, Kiritsis held Hall at gunpoint for 63 hours before finally releasing him unharmed. At his trial, Kiritsis was found not guilty by reason of insanity.

And in 1978, four young employees of a Burger Chef restaurant in Speedway disappeared. Their bodies were found the next day in a wooded area of Johnson County. The murders were never solved.

By the late '70s, the economy was struggling with both inflation and recession. Large plants, such as Western Electric and Chrysler, which employed thousands, were soon to shut down.

Lugar had served two terms as mayor and was succeeded by William Hudnut, who shared the vision for what Downtown could become. Lugar's success had been to give the community a modern government structure, while Hudnut's early focus was to develop the Indianapolis economy. He seized on opportunities to expand the city's hospital system, pushed the city as a distribution center and enhanced Indianapolis as a convention site and sports center.

A revitalized Downtown still seemed like a pipe dream, and the poor economy did not provide much fuel for big projects. But near the end of the decade, in 1978, a little project to beautify Monument Circle won the hearts of the city. In those days the Circle was a place where the buses turned around and the Soldiers and Sailors Monument was off-limits to frivolous activities such as eating your lunch. That would change, brick by brick.

Opposite page: Women's liberation march through Indianapolis, August 1971.

Above, left: John Florence (with sign), Brunetta Fowler and Jerry Chambers are shown at a planning meeting for the 1973 Indiana Black Expo.

Above, right: President Richard M. Nixon's admirers crowd in to shake his hand during his visit to Indianapolis on Feb. 5, 1970.

Left: Karen Thrasher (right) gets a pamphlet containing voter information from Barbara Crowe, an Urban League "voter-ette," on Monument Circle, October 1972.

Right: An integrated freshman class from Crispus Attucks attend school at the Tudor Hall School. The school was a compromise for an integration order, white resistance to attend the old Attucks and blacks wanting to continue the tradition of the all-black school. The integrated freshman class attended school in the former Tudor Hall school for girls — which had earlier merged with the Park School for boys to form Park Tudor school.

Above: Thousands attend the opening of the new Indiana Convention Center, located in downtown Indianapolis, May 1972.

Above: The Aug. 9, 1974, edition of The Indianapolis Star.

Left: Rev. Jacqueline Means stands during a tribute to her from the pulpit of All Saints Episcopal Church, January 1977. Means became the first woman priest in the Episcopal Church. She was ordained at All Saints Episcopal Church.

Right: Indianapolis Mayor Richard G. Lugar, October 1973.

Below: State Senator Julia Carson and Representative William Crawford discuss a bill in the Indiana General Assembly on Feb. 1, 1977.

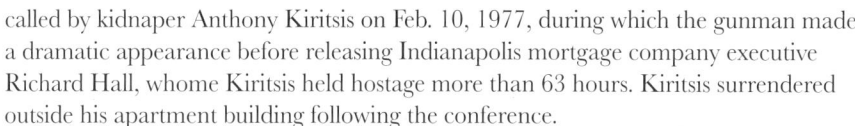

Left: Anthony Kiritsis holds a sawed-off 12-guage shotgun to the head of Indianapolis mortgage company executive Richard Hall as they walk along Washington Street shortly after Hall was kidnaped from his office at 129 E. Market.

Right: Crowded scene at the news conference called by kidnaper Anthony Kiritsis on Feb. 10, 1977, during which the gunman made a dramatic appearance before releasing Indianapolis mortgage company executive Richard Hall, whome Kiritsis held hostage more than 63 hours. Kiritsis surrendered outside his apartment building following the conference.

Below, left: With a shotgun still wired to his neck, mortgage firm executive Dick Hall reads a statement as his captor, Anthony G. Kiritsis, keeps a ring of police and reporters at bay. The drama, televised live to satisfy the gunman's demands, brought indignant phone calls from viewers – most of them angry because Kiritsis' vulgar language was broadcast, not concerned that a potential murderer was appearing on their screens. A short time later, Kiritsis released Hall, fired into the ceiling and was arrested.

Below: Anthony Kiritsis taken into custody after the news conference.

Above: The May 39, 1977, edition of The Indianapolis Star.

Above: The Jan. 27, 1978, edition of The Indianapolis Star.

Left: Basketball isn't the only sport Larry Bird played for Indiana State. Here, with a plug of tobacco in his cheek, the Sycamore first baseman warms up for a game in 1979.

Right: Ann Meyers, 24, the first woman asked to try out for an NBA team, participates in a workout with the Indiana Pacers as the rookie/free agent camp opened at Hinkle Fieldhouse on Sept. 10, 1979.

Below, left: Rev. James W. Jones, while pastor of the People's Temple Christian Church at 975 N. Delaware, was appointed to the Indianapolis Human Rights Commission in 1961 by Mayor Charles H. Boswell.

Below, right: Scene of death on Nov. 18, 1978, in which more than 900 members of the Peoples Temple died in the mass murder-suicide in Jonestown, Guyana. The Rev. Jim Jones, leader of the church and a former Indianapolis minister, died along with his followers.

A City Transformed
1980 - 1989

In the 1980s, the ambitions of city planners were stunningly fulfilled as Downtown Indianapolis experienced the most sweeping changes since the 1920s.

Those involved would later look back on 1982 as the year when two pivotal events took place. One was the construction of the American United Life tower and the other was the city's successful hosting of the National Sports Festival. Both were the result of months, or years, of effort by city officials and both sparked continuing success.

The city had spent 18 months pursuing AUL before the insurance company decided to build its headquarters downtown.

When it opened, the AUL Building was briefly the city's tallest structure, but the Bank One Tower would soon surpass it. At least six other office buildings went up as well. Had the AUL deal fallen through, some of those projects might not have happened either.

When the Hilton on the Circle (which later became the Radisson) opened in 1970, it was the first major hotel to open Downtown in nearly 50 years. But during the '80s, 1,700 new hotel rooms were completed. Several historic preservation districts were also created as preservationists laid claim to an area that stretched roughly from Fountain Square on the Southeastside north to 22nd Street in the Herron-Morton district.

Renovation revived Monument Circle, the Indiana and Walker theater buildings and the Lockerbie Hotel, which was transformed into the lavish Canterbury Hotel.

Union Station was brought back to life as a festival-style marketplace with shops and restaurants. The Indianapolis Zoo spread its wings in White River State Park, and work began on a retail complex to be called Circle Centre.

On the near Westside, the campus buildings of IUPUI seemed to sprout out of the ground like mushrooms. The Hoosier Dome, with its distinctive inflatable roof, quickly found a new tenant — the former Baltimore Colts.

Opposite page: A view of Indianapolis looking northeast across the eight-acre fabric roof of the recently constructed Hoosier Dome, July 1987.

It was no accident that Colts owner Robert Irsay chose Indianapolis. Mayor William Hudnut and other city officials had courted Irsay as early as 1978. The Hoosier Dome (later re-named the RCA Dome) was built with NFL football in mind, but planners insisted it be viable if necessary on conventions and concerts alone.

Sports wasn't just a weekend diversion anymore. It was a new industry – and a pollution-free one at that – which city planners had begun nurturing the previous decade.

As part of the 1978 Amateur Sports Act, Congress required that national governing bodies be established for nearly 40 sports. Those organizations had to be headquartered somewhere, so why not Indianapolis? The Indiana Sports Corporation was created in 1979 to turn that idea into a reality.

If the city wanted to pursue multi-sport events, it needed some unique or world-class facilities in some of the sports. Out of that came the Track and Field Stadium ($5.9 million) and the Natatorium ($21.5 million), both at IUPUI.

When the city successfully hosted the National Sports Festival in 1982, it was both the culmination of that early planning and the beginning of a new identity for a city that had been described as a cemetery with lights and given the nickname "India-noplace".

Then came the Colts in 1984 and the announcement that Indianapolis would be the host city for the 1987 Pan American Games. In 1985, the city reveled in a Newsweek story that labeled Indianapolis the Cinderella of the Rust Belt.

Things had happened so fast that some advocated a breather. In 1980, the city had created a regional center plan that was supposed to guide Downtown development until 2000. Yet within six or seven years, it was essentially completed. Why not slow down?

But there was one piece of the puzzle not yet in place – the Downtown mall.

Above: Senator Birch Bayh, accompanied by his son Evan Bayh, concedes the 1980 Senate race to Dan Quayle. Bayh was a three-term Senator, who twice ran for president.

Right: Construction of the AUL Tower in 1981. The tower is the headquarters for American United Life.

Above: Sports legend Larry Bird shares a laugh with longtime fan and former French Lick neighbor Mildred Quinn during his first visit to MSA as a Boston Celtic when they played the Indiana Pacers on Dec. 1, 1981. The Pacers beat the Celtics, 90-87.

Left: Runners jam Monument Circle moments before the start of the fifth annual "500" Festival Mini-Marathon in 1981. Hundreds of spectators crowded the Circle and sidewalks near the starting line for 30 minutes of festivities before the start of the 13.1-mile race over city streets to the Indianapolis Motor Speedway.

Left: More than 2,600 athletes parade across Obelisk Square in downtown Indianapolis for the opening of the National Sports Festival in 1982.

Right: Skater Natalie Seybold goes aloft as National Sports Festival athletes parade across Obelisk Square in 1982.

Below: Heavyweights Charles Barkley (left) of the South and Michael Brown (17) of the East wrestle for the ball at Market Square Arena during the National Sports Festival's gold-medal basketball game, August 1982.

Above: 350,000 square yards of fabric, weighing more than a half-million pounds, were pushed into place by air to form the roof of the Hoosier Dome during its construction in 1983. At its highest point, the roof is 193 feet above the playing floor of the 63,000-seat stadium. Teflon-coated roof panels are attached to more than 2 miles of cables, but the roof is held in place by air pressure. It took about 45 minutes to inflate the $6.1 million roof.

Above: The March 30, 1984, edition of The Indianapolis Star.

Above: Governor Robert Orr visits Moorhead Elementary School on Feb. 14, 1985, and is interviewed by Mindy Wagoner, 7, a first-grader.

Below: Robert Irsay (left) and Indianapolis Mayor William H. Hudnut in a victory clinch following the Indianapolis Colts arrival in town, during a ceremony at the Hoosier Dome on April 2, 1984.

Above: In 1986, a renovated Union Station, the former center of rail travel in the city, opened as a festival marketplace, filled with stores, restaurants and nightclubs.

Chapter Nine ~ 1980-1989

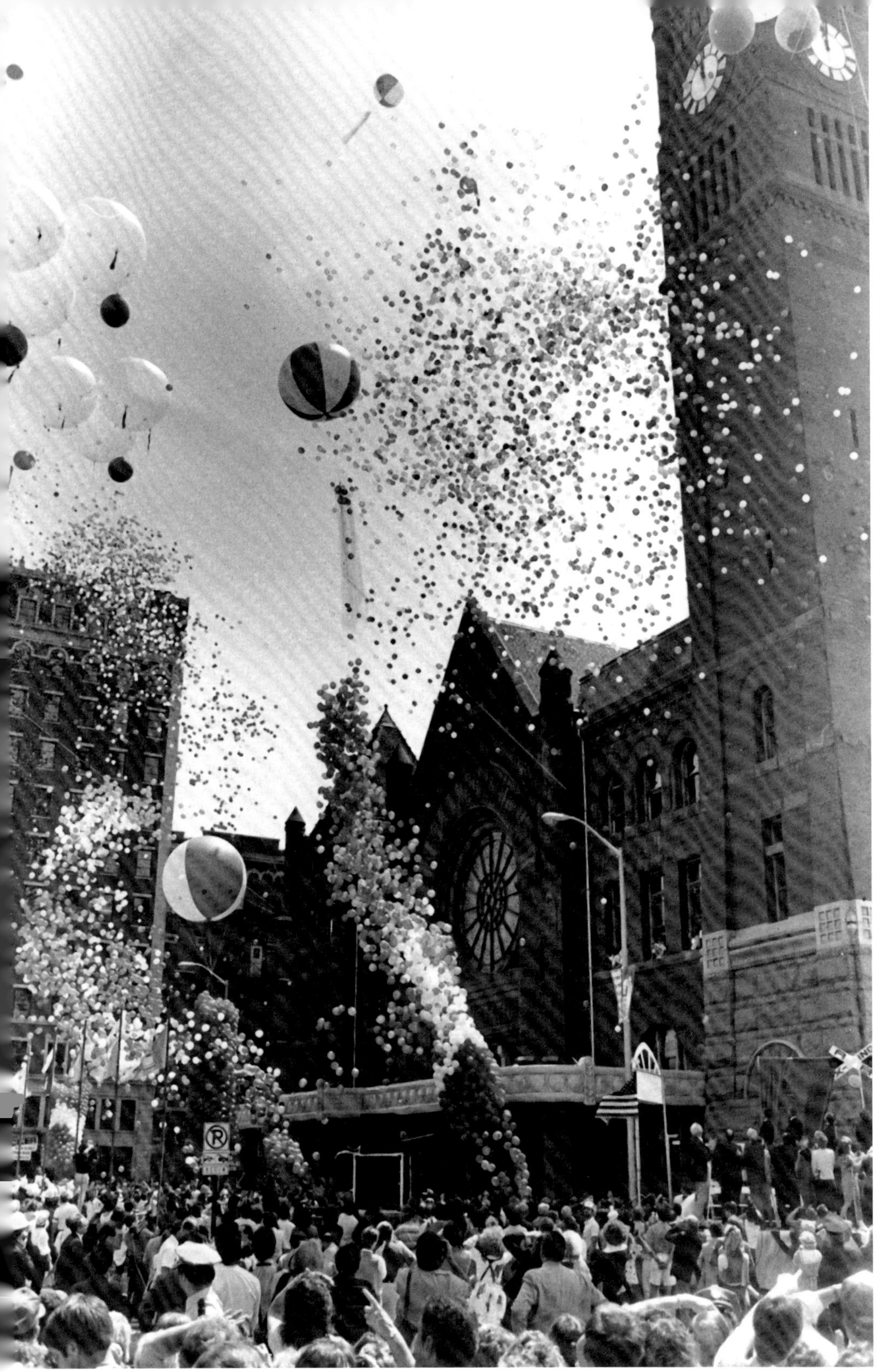

Above: Balloons go up at the reopening of Union Station in 1986.

Partly cloudy
Partly cloudy with a chance of morning flurries. High, 30.

THE INDIANAPOLIS STAR

Chuckle
Alarm clock: a mechanical device used to wake up people who have no children.

WEDNESDAY, JANUARY 29, 1986 — "Where the Spirit of the Lord is, there is Liberty" II Cor. 3:17 — ☆ ☆ ☆ ☆ — Single Copy 25 Cents

Ocean search reveals no evidence any of 7 aboard shuttle survived

ASSOCIATED PRESS

Challenger's mission ends in ball of fire 10 miles up. Shuttle exploded 72 seconds after liftoff, killing 7.

Explosion is worst space age tragedy

By EDWARD K. DeLONG
UNITED PRESS INTERNATIONAL

Cape Canaveral, Fla. — The shuttle Challenger exploded in a boiling ball of flame 72 seconds after blastoff Tuesday, killing teacher Sharon Christa McAuliffe and her six crewmates in the worst space tragedy since man began reaching for the stars 25 years ago.

Ships, planes and helicopters rushed to a vast area 50 miles off the Florida coast, where flaming debris rained down for half an hour after the mighty explosion, but all they found were parts of Challenger's booster rockets.

"I regret that I have to report that based on very preliminary searches of the ocean where Challenger impacted this morning, these searches have not revealed any evidence that the crew of the Challenger survived," said Jesse Moore, chief of the shuttle program, five hours after the explosion.

The shuttle, loaded at launch with nearly a half million gallons of explosive hydrogen and oxygen, carried no emergency escape system.

It was 10 miles high when it erupted into flames. The earth-shaking roar of blastoff had subsided and the majestic contrail following Challenger into space turned silently into a serpent of smoke and fire writhing across the sky.

Wife wants program to go on

On board the Challenger were commander Francis "Dick" Scobee, 46, co-pilot Michael J. Smith, 40, Judith Resnik, 36, Ellison S. Onizuka, 39, Ronald E. McNair, 35, satellite engineer Gregory B. Jarvis, 41, and Mrs. McAuliffe, the 37-year-old Concord, N.H., social studies teacher picked from 11,000 candidates to be the first private citizen in space. They were the first Americans to die on a mission into space.

"It's been nearly a quarter of a century that we thought this might happen sometime," said U.S. Sen. John Glenn, who in 1962 became the first American to orbit the Earth. "We hoped that day would never come. Unfortunately it has."

Cries of horror went up at viewing sites along the coast when the shuttle exploded at 11:39 a.m. EST, spewing burning pieces like a massive fireworks display. A shocked nation watched the replays moments later on television.

Mrs. McAuliffe's husband, Steven, and two children Caroline, 6, and Scott, 9, watched the disaster that claimed the teacher's life but were hurried away immediately by NASA officials.

Vice President George Bush, dispatched to the Kennedy Space Center by President Reagan, arrived at dusk with Glenn and Sen. Jake Garn, R-Utah, who flew a shuttle mission last year.

"The President and I and the entire nation join in mourning the seven splendid men and women who now rest in God's arms," Bush said.

"I don't know anytime that I have been so shocked and so moved since my first wife was killed in a car accident," Garn said, choking back tears. "It is very difficult for me personally when you lose so many friends all at once."

Late Tuesday night Garn emerged from a meeting with the families of Challenger's crew and said Scobee's wife, speaking for all of them, asked that the tragedy not be allowed to harm the future of the space program.

Rep. Bill Nelson, D-Fla., who returned from a flight aboard the shuttle Columbia only 10 days ago, said "Pioneers have had tragedy before and tragedy will occur again." Computer engineer Richard Prickett said "There was a lot of crying" in launch control. "Everybody sort of takes this personally. You can't be part of the program and not feel some responsibility."

Ships search through night

Night fell over the coast in a cloudless pink sunset and the five planes and eight helicopters scouring an area 58 miles wide by 115 miles long were recalled, to begin their search patterns again at first light. The ships in the search continued patrolling through the night.

The Atlantic in that area ranges from 75 to 200 feet deep. An Air Force officer said the largest piece of debris seen so far was only 2 feet wide and 5 to 10 feet long.

"The first thing we wanted to do was pick up survivors," Air Force spokesman Col. John Shults said about seven hours after the explosion. "That's now probably out of the question. Now we want to pick up the debris. Some of it may be covered with toxic chemicals, so we're warning civilians not to pick anything up."

Challenger was hurtling toward space at nearly 2,000

See SHUTTLE Page 12

LIFTOFF TO DISASTER

Index

Phone numbers

Circulation	633-9211
Main office	633-1240
Classified Ads	633-1212
Scores after 4:30 p.m.	633-1200

Coupons offer savings

The Indianapolis Star today contains at least 33 coupons, which readers can clip and redeem to save money. There were 217 coupons in *The Star* last week, redeemable at a value of $87.15.

Prayer

When we can let one word or one action help another to keep going one more day, Lord, thank You for leading us to those who are looking for renewed hope. Amen.

VOLUME 83, No. 238
CARRIER DELIVERED $1.20 PER WK
MOTOR DELIVERED $1.25 PER WK

'We'll continue'

Reagan promises more flights, delays speech

By NORMAN D. SANDLER
UNITED PRESS INTERNATIONAL

Washington — President Reagan scrapped his State of the Union speech Tuesday to mourn the crew of the shuttle Challenger as fallen heroes and he promised, "We'll continue our quest in space. . . . Nothing ends here."

"The future doesn't belong to the faint-hearted. It belongs to the brave," Mr. Reagan said in a nationally televised late-afternoon address from the Oval Office, less than six hours after the spacecraft blew up. "The Challenger crew was pulling us into the future, and we'll continue to follow."

Leading the nation in mourning, Mr. Reagan postponed his fifth State of the Union address to Congress for a week. Instead he spoke somberly about the explosion that shattered Challenger and left no evidence of survivors among its seven-member crew — including the first teacher in space, Sharon Christa McAuliffe.

Mr. Reagan, for whom Tuesday was to have kicked off an aggressive weeklong campaign to promote his political agenda for 1986, said the day instead had been transformed into one "of mourning and remembering."

"Nancy and I are pained to the core by the tragedy of the shuttle Challenger," he said. "We know we share this pain with all of the people of this country. This is truly a national loss."

About nine hours before his scheduled appearance before

See REAGAN Page 12

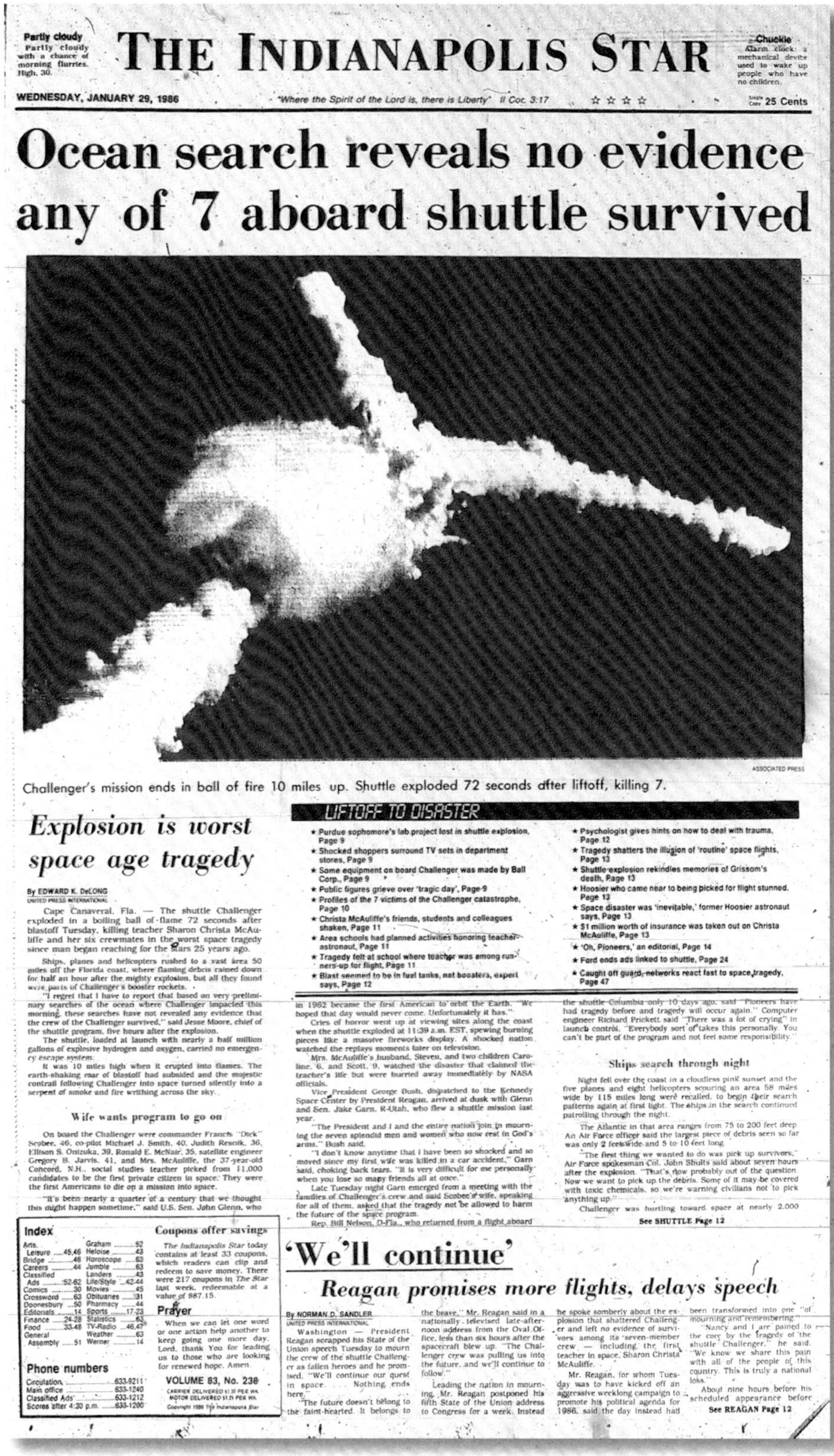

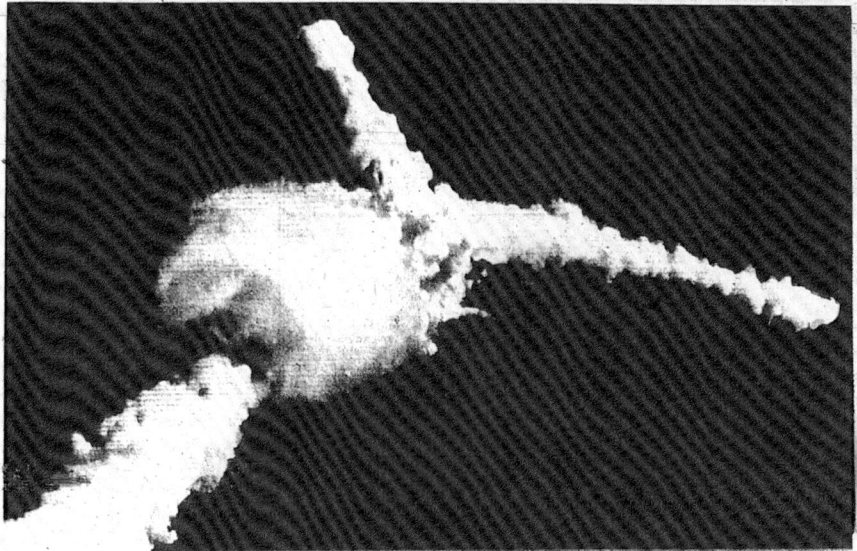

Above: The Jan. 29, 1986, edition of The Indianapolis Star.

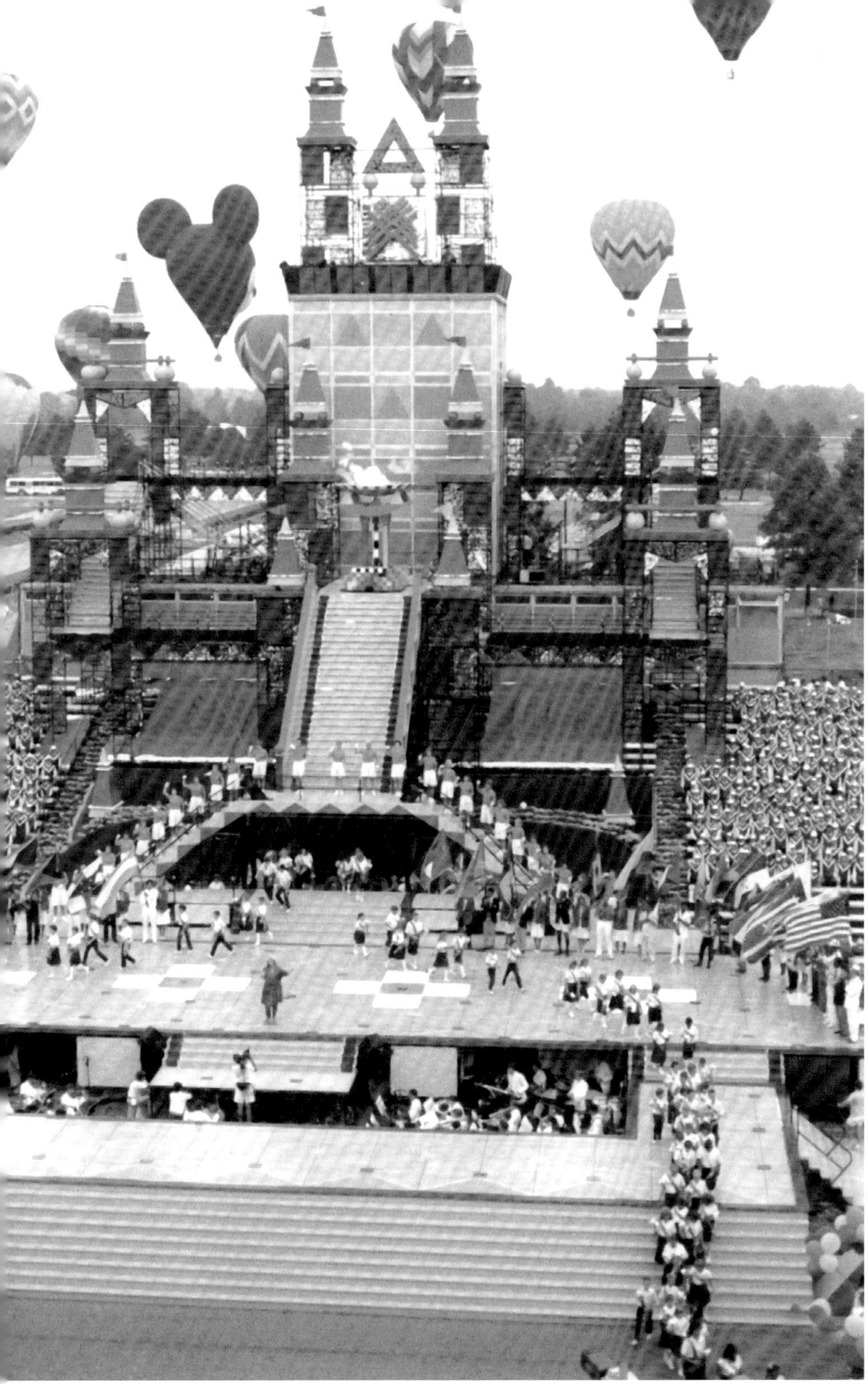

Above: Nearly 80,000 spectators and athletes attended the opening ceremonies of the Pan American Games at the Indianapolis Motor Speedway on Aug. 8, 1987. For three weeks, over 4,000 athletes from 38 Pan American countries competed in 30 sporting events.

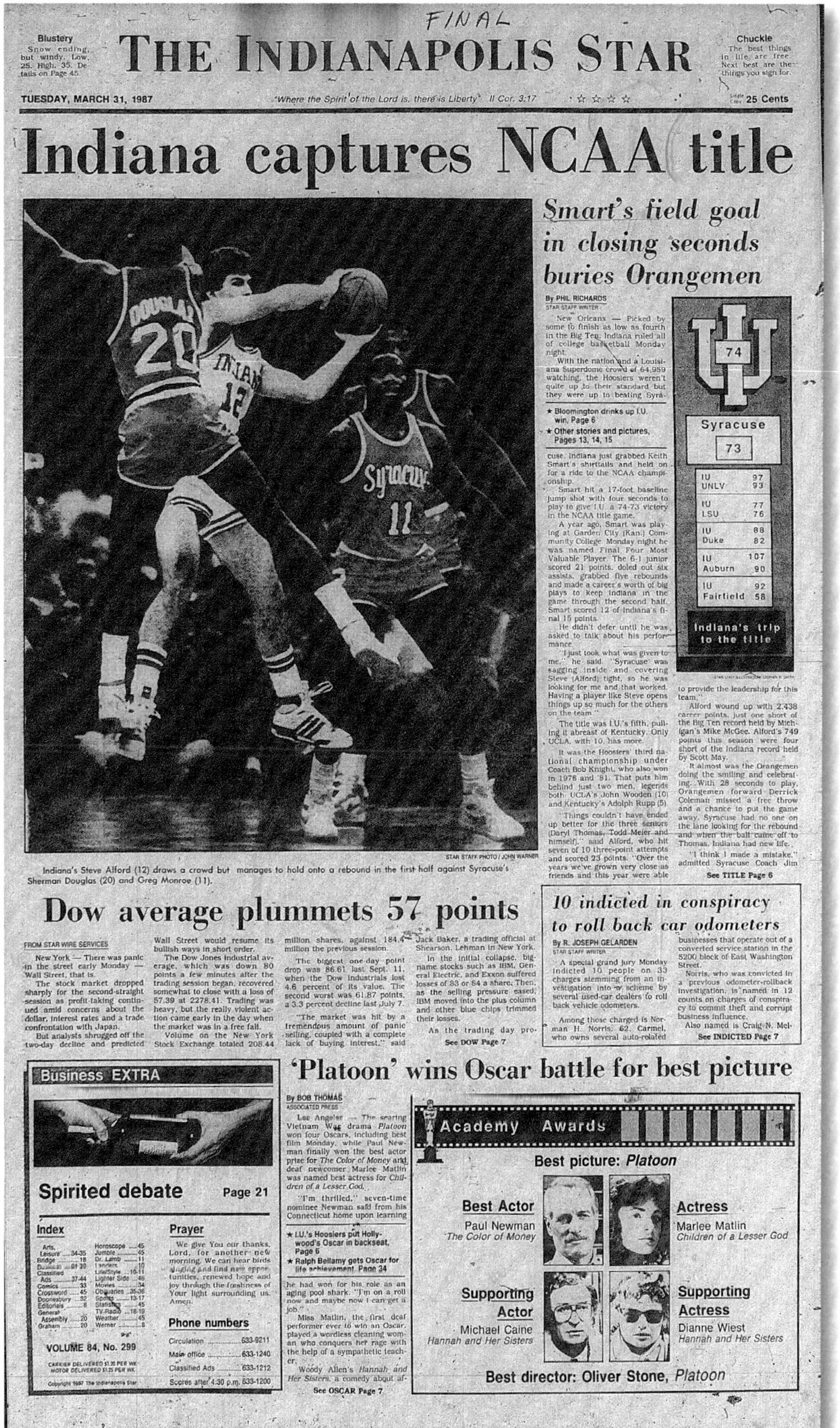

Blustery
Snow ending, but windy. Low, 25. High, 35. Details on Page 45.

THE INDIANAPOLIS STAR

Chuckle
The best things in life are free. Next best are the things you sign for.

TUESDAY, MARCH 31, 1987 — "Where the Spirit of the Lord is, there is Liberty" II Cor. 3:17 — ☆ ☆ ☆ ☆ — Single Copy 25 Cents

Indiana captures NCAA title

Indiana's Steve Alford (12) draws a crowd but manages to hold onto a rebound in the first half against Syracuse's Sherman Douglas (20) and Greg Monroe (11).

STAR STAFF PHOTO / JOHN WARNER

Smart's field goal in closing seconds buries Orangemen

By PHIL RICHARDS
STAR STAFF WRITER

New Orleans — Picked by some to finish as low as fourth in the Big Ten, Indiana ruled all of college basketball Monday night.

With the nation and a Louisiana Superdome crowd of 64,959 watching, the Hoosiers weren't quite up to their standard but they were up to beating Syracuse. Indiana just grabbed Keith Smart's shirttails and held on for a ride to the NCAA championship.

★ Bloomington drinks up I.U. win, Page 6
★ Other stories and pictures, Pages 13, 14, 15

Smart hit a 17-foot baseline jump shot with four seconds to play to give I.U. a 74-73 victory in the NCAA title game.

A year ago, Smart was playing at Garden City (Kan.) Community College. Monday night he was named Final Four Most Valuable Player. The 6-1 junior scored 21 points, doled out six assists, grabbed five rebounds and made a career's worth of big plays to keep Indiana in the game through the second half. Smart scored 12 of Indiana's final 15 points.

He didn't defer until he was asked to talk about his performance.

"I just took what was given to me," he said. "Syracuse was sagging inside and covering Steve (Alford) tight, so he was looking for me and that worked. Having a player like Steve opens things up so much for the others on the team."

The title was I.U.'s fifth, pulling it abreast of Kentucky. Only UCLA, with 10, has more.

It was the Hoosiers' third national championship under Coach Bob Knight, who also won in 1976 and '81. That puts him behind just two men, legends both: UCLA's John Wooden (10) and Kentucky's Adolph Rupp (5).

"Things couldn't have ended up better for the three seniors (Daryl Thomas, Todd Meier and himself)," said Alford, who hit seven of 10 three-point attempts and scored 23 points. "Over the years we've grown very close as friends and this year were able to provide the leadership for this team."

Alford wound up with 2,438 career points, just one short of the Big Ten record held by Michigan's Mike McGee. Alford's 749 points this season were four short of the Indiana record held by Scott May.

It almost was the Orangemen doing the smiling and celebrating. With 28 seconds to play, Orangemen forward Derrick Coleman missed a free throw and a chance to put the game away. Syracuse had no one on the lane looking for the rebound and when the ball came off to Thomas, Indiana had new life.

"I think I made a mistake," admitted Syracuse Coach Jim

See TITLE Page 6

IU 74
Syracuse 73

IU	97
UNLV	93
IU	77
LSU	76
IU	88
Duke	82
IU	107
Auburn	90
IU	92
Fairfield	58

Indiana's trip to the title

Dow average plummets 57 points

FROM STAR WIRE SERVICES

New York — There was panic in the street early Monday — Wall Street, that is.

The stock market dropped sharply for the second-straight session as profit-taking continued amid concerns about the dollar, interest rates and a trade confrontation with Japan.

But analysts shrugged off the two-day decline and predicted Wall Street would resume its bullish ways in short order.

The Dow Jones industrial average, which was down 80 points a few minutes after the trading session began, recovered somewhat to close with a loss of 57.39 at 2278.41. Trading was heavy, but the really violent action came early in the day when the market was in a free fall.

Volume on the New York Stock Exchange totaled 208.44 million shares, against 184.4 million the previous session.

The biggest one-day point drop was 86.61 last Sept. 11, when the Dow industrials lost 4.6 percent of its value. The second worst was 61.87 points, a 3.3 percent decline last July 7.

"The market was hit by a tremendous amount of panic selling, coupled with a complete lack of buying interest," said Jack Baker, a trading official at Shearson, Lehman in New York.

In the initial collapse, big-name stocks such as IBM, General Electric, and Exxon suffered losses of $3 or $4 a share. Then, as the selling pressure eased, IBM moved into the plus column and other blue chips trimmed their losses.

As the trading day pro-

See DOW Page 7

10 indicted in conspiracy to roll back car odometers

By R. JOSEPH GELARDEN
STAR STAFF WRITER

A special grand jury Monday indicted 10 people on 33 charges stemming from an investigation into a scheme by several used-car dealers to roll back vehicle odometers.

Among those charged is Norman H. Norris, 62, Carmel, who owns several auto-related businesses that operate out of a converted service station in the 5200 block of East Washington Street.

Norris, who was convicted in a previous odometer-rollback investigation, is named in 12 counts on charges of conspiracy to commit theft and corrupt business influence.

Also named is Craig N. Mel-

See INDICTED Page 7

Business EXTRA

Spirited debate Page 21

Index

Prayer

We give You our thanks, Lord, for another new morning. We can hear birds singing and find new opportunities, renewed hope and joy through the freshness of Your light surrounding us. Amen.

Phone numbers

Circulation	633-9211
Main office	633-1240
Classified Ads	633-1212
Scores after 4:30 p.m.	633-1200

VOLUME 84, No. 299

CARRIER DELIVERED $1.20 PER WK
MOTOR DELIVERED $1.25 PER WK

'Platoon' wins Oscar battle for best picture

By BOB THOMAS
ASSOCIATED PRESS

Los Angeles — The searing Vietnam War drama *Platoon* won four Oscars, including best film Monday, while Paul Newman finally won the best actor prize for *The Color of Money* and deaf newcomer Marlee Matlin was named best actress for *Children of a Lesser God*.

"I'm thrilled," seven-time nominee Newman said from his Connecticut home upon learning he had won for his role as an aging pool shark. "I'm on a roll now and maybe now I can get a job."

★ I.U.'s Hoosiers put Hollywood's Oscar in backseat, Page 6
★ Ralph Bellamy gets Oscar for life achievement, Page 34

Miss Matlin, the first deaf performer ever to win an Oscar, played a wordless cleaning woman who conquers her rage with the help of a sympathetic teacher.

Woody Allen's *Hannah and Her Sisters*, a comedy about af-

See OSCAR Page 7

Academy Awards

Best picture: *Platoon*

Best Actor
Paul Newman
The Color of Money

Actress
Marlee Matlin
Children of a Lesser God

Supporting Actor
Michael Caine
Hannah and Her Sisters

Supporting Actress
Dianne Wiest
Hannah and Her Sisters

Best director: Oliver Stone, *Platoon*

Above: The March 31, 1987, edition of The Indianapolis Star.

Above: Crowds stream through the gates of the new Indianapolis Zoo after ribbon-cutting ceremonies were completed, June 1988.

Right: Government and civic officials take part in the topping-out ceremony for the two-story Eiteljorg Museum of the American Indian and Western Art under construction in White River State Park in 1988. Harrison Eiteljorg (left), who donated his collection to form the core of the museum's collection, signs the beam as Mayor William H. Hudnut watches.

Below: Deer Creek Music Center opened in 1989 in Hamilton County. The facility features a stage amphitheater on 220 acres with seating for over 20,000. The center changed it's name in 2000 to the Verizon Wireless Music Center.

Above: The Nov. 10, 1989, edition of The Indianapolis Star.

Chapter Nine ~ 1980-1989 111

A New Millennium
1990 - 2003

During the last decade of the 20th Century the city of Indianapolis brought to completion more than two decades of planning with the construction of the tallest building Downtown and the opening of the Circle Centre Mall that became its centerpiece.

From its offices at 307 N. Pennsylvania Street, The Indianapolis Star had chronicled and photographed the rapid changes taking place all around it. By the century's end, The Star too would be swept up in change.

The 1990s began with completion of the Bank One Tower, which at 51 stories became the city's tallest building. But the city's most ambitious project, the downtown mall, seemed headed for trouble.

In March 1989, Mayor William Hudnut had jumped aboard a wrecking crane and sent its ball smashing into a building at 25 W. Washington Street to symbolically begin construction of the mall. But taking down the old buildings was the easy part. Putting up new ones was another matter, particularly at the scale that had been envisioned. The economy had slowed down and progress on the mall slowed with it.

For a few years, Downtown workers were accustomed to the sight of gaping holes in the ground and facades held up with steel beams.

The city's two home-grown department stores, L.S. Ayres and Wm. H. Blocks, had once been envisioned as the anchors of any downtown mall that might be built. But by the 1990s, both were gone.

Hudnut left office after a remarkable four terms as mayor and was succeeded in 1992 by fellow Republican Stephen Goldsmith, who was less enthusiastic about the mall project and even halted construction for a time. But he later dropped his opposition and the mall was finally completed, opening with great fanfare in 1995.

The following year, the Indianapolis Indians began playing at their new Downtown ballpark, Victory Field, and in 1997 ground was broken Downtown for the Indiana Pacers' new home, Conseco Fieldhouse. In the late 1990s, the Pacers, led by clutch shooter Reggie Miller, were contending in the post-season almost every year and in 2000 would make it all the way to the NBA Finals, losing the championship game to the overpowering LA Lakers.

Changes were also in the works at the city's most famous sports venue, the Indianapolis Motor Speedway. For as long as anyone could remember, IMS had hosted only one auto race a year, the Indianapolis 500. In the 1990s, under the leadership of Tony Hulman George, IMS developed two additional annual racing events. The Brickyard 400 was launched in 1994 and additional track was constructed to accommodate an annual Formula One race, which was held for the first time in 2000.

George also formed the Indy Racing League, prompting a split with team owners associated with Championship Auto Racing Teams, particularly those owned by Roger Penske. For the latter half of the 1990s, some of the best drivers and teams in open-wheel racing boycotted the Indianapolis 500 and "the Greatest Spectacle in Racing" looked in danger of losing its stature in the world of auto racing. But after a few years the rift was healed and Penske drivers returned to Indianapolis.

As it covered these and other events of the 1990s — winning the Pulitzer Prize in 1991 — The Indianapolis Star was going through a transformation of its own. From the 1940s until his death in 1975, Eugene C. Pulliam had owned and personally operated The Star and the city's afternoon paper, The Indianapolis News. His son, Eugene S. Pulliam, succeeded him as publisher, but ownership passed to a trust governed by a board that included family members and company executives.

The days when a single individual owned and operated a big city newspaper were largely over and, like other industries, most media companies were evolving into large public corporations answerable to shareholders. In 1989, The Star's parent company, Central Newspapers Inc., issued public stock for the first time and, in 1995, the newsrooms of the once-competing Star and News were blended into one staff. The national trend was also toward morning newspapers and, in 1999, The News ceased publishing.

Also in 1999, Eugene S. Pulliam died, and for the first time in half a century no Pulliam sat in the publisher's office. Although The Star and CNI were financially healthy, surviving family members and trustees knew it would be difficult to remain independent in the new era of media conglomerates. In June 2000, it was announced that the company would be acquired by the Gannett Company, the nation's largest newspaper group.

In 2003, the city of Indianapolis again looks toward a new century with optimism in its ability to face whatever the future might bring. The Star will be here to cover it.

Opposite page: In 1907 a building was erected at the corner of Pennsylvania and New York streets (inset) and became the home of The Indianapolis Star. Over the years, The Star Building expanded and now encompasses the entire city block. The Newsroom and business operations remain downtown; however, the printing press is now located in the Pulliam Production Center on the city's northside. In July 2002, The Star made a substantial investment in its future with the unveiling of its $72 million state-of-the-art production facility. The seven-story press is housed here.

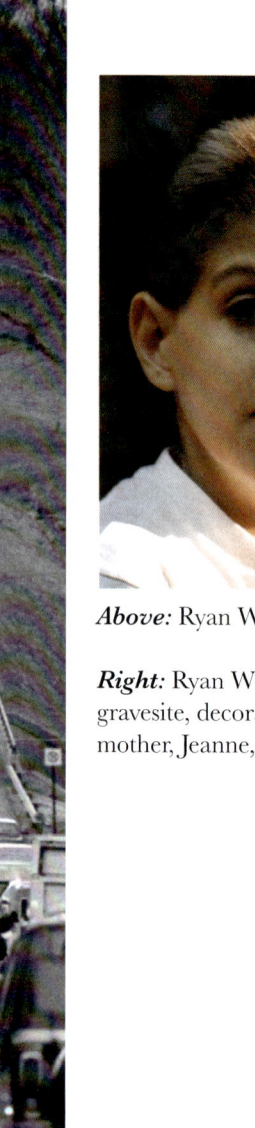

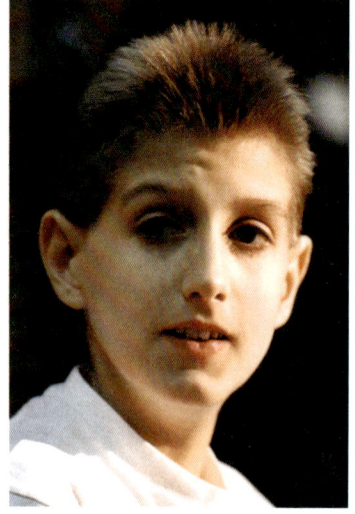

Above: Ryan White in 1987.

Right: Ryan White's Cicero gravesite, decorated by his mother, Jeanne, Oct. 1990.

Above: Motorcycle police lead hundreds of cars in the procession to the cemetery after the funeral service of Ryan White, April 11, 1990. White died after a lengthy and highly publicized battle with AIDS. Shunned from his school in Kokomo because of the disease and welcomed by another school in Hamilton County, his plight was covered by the media. His funeral was attended by athletes, celebrities and first lady Barbara Bush.

Right: Indianapolis Star Publisher Eugene S. Pulliam and reporters Susan Headden and Joe Hallinan react to the news that they have won the Pulitzer Prize for their series on medical malpractice. 1991.

Above: A firefighter hoses the wreckage of a plane crash in Greenwood that killed Indianapolis civic leaders, Frank McKinney Jr., Michael Carroll, Robert V. Welch and John Weliever, Sept. 11, 1992.

Below: Homeowner Paula Deane (sitting) chats with neighbors Pam and William Harvey as Elmer Killmon looks at the wreckage, September 1992.

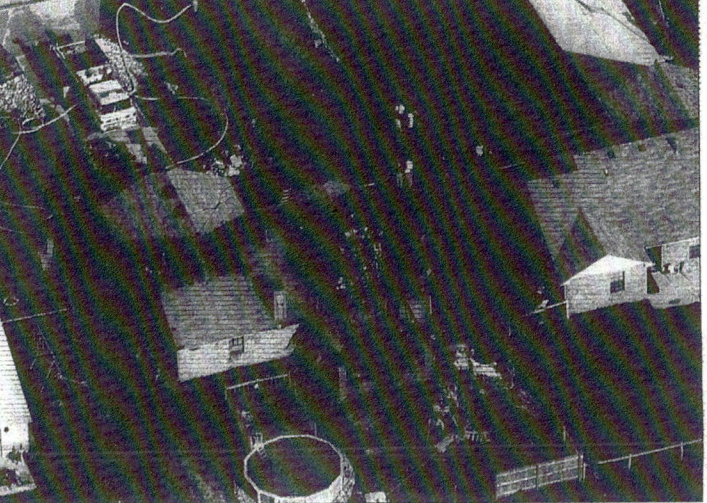

Above: The Sept. 12, 1992, edition of The Indianapolis Star.

Above: A trombonist from Gary's Theodore Roosevelt High School marching band shows his enthusiasm during the 1994 Circle City Classic Parade.

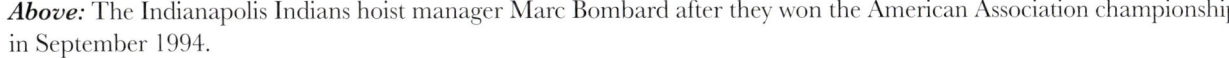

Above: The Indianapolis Indians hoist manager Marc Bombard after they won the American Association championship in September 1994.

Above, right: The Indianapolis Ice celebrate their championship in the early 1990s.

Right: Pacers players joke around at a rally at City Market in 1994 honoring the teams' accomplishments in the NBA playoffs. The Pacers fell just short of the NBA finals.

Chapter Ten ~ 1990-1999

Above: Boxer Mike Tyson comes down the stairway in the City-County Building after leaving the courtroom with police guards on Feb. 10. 1992. Tyson was convicted for raping beauty pageant contestant Desiree Washington in the Canterbury Hotel on July 19, 1991, and served nearly three years of a six-year prison sentence in a Plainfield prison.

Above: Jeff Gordon celebrates on top of his racecar after winning the first NASCAR Brickyard 400 at the Indianapolis Motor Speedway on Aug. 6, 1994.

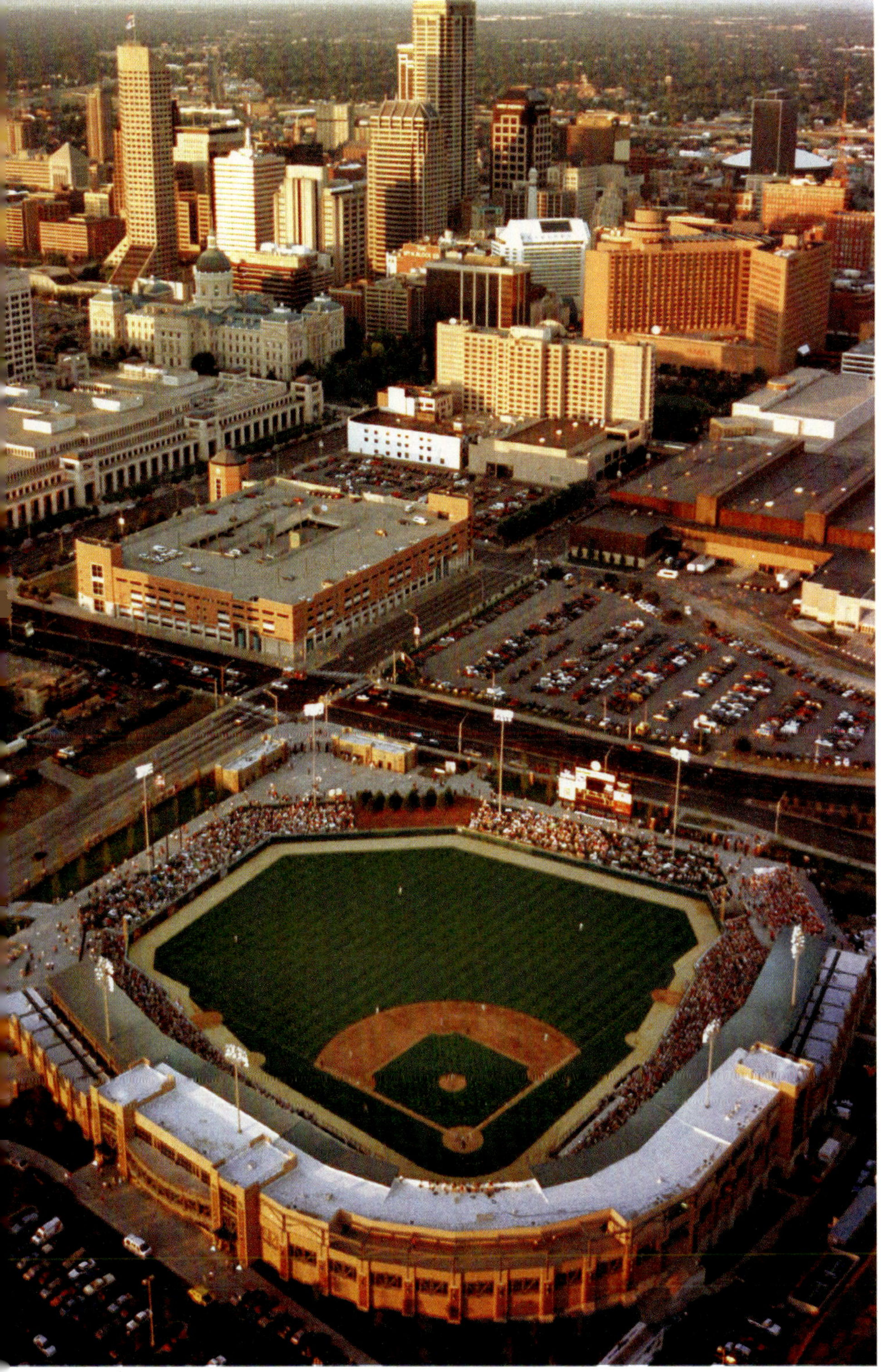

Above: Aerial view of Victory Field, July 11, 1996. Often referred to as "the most beautiful ballpark in the country", Victory Field is the home of the minor league Indianapolis Indians. The $18 million ballpark features a stunning view of the city's skyline.

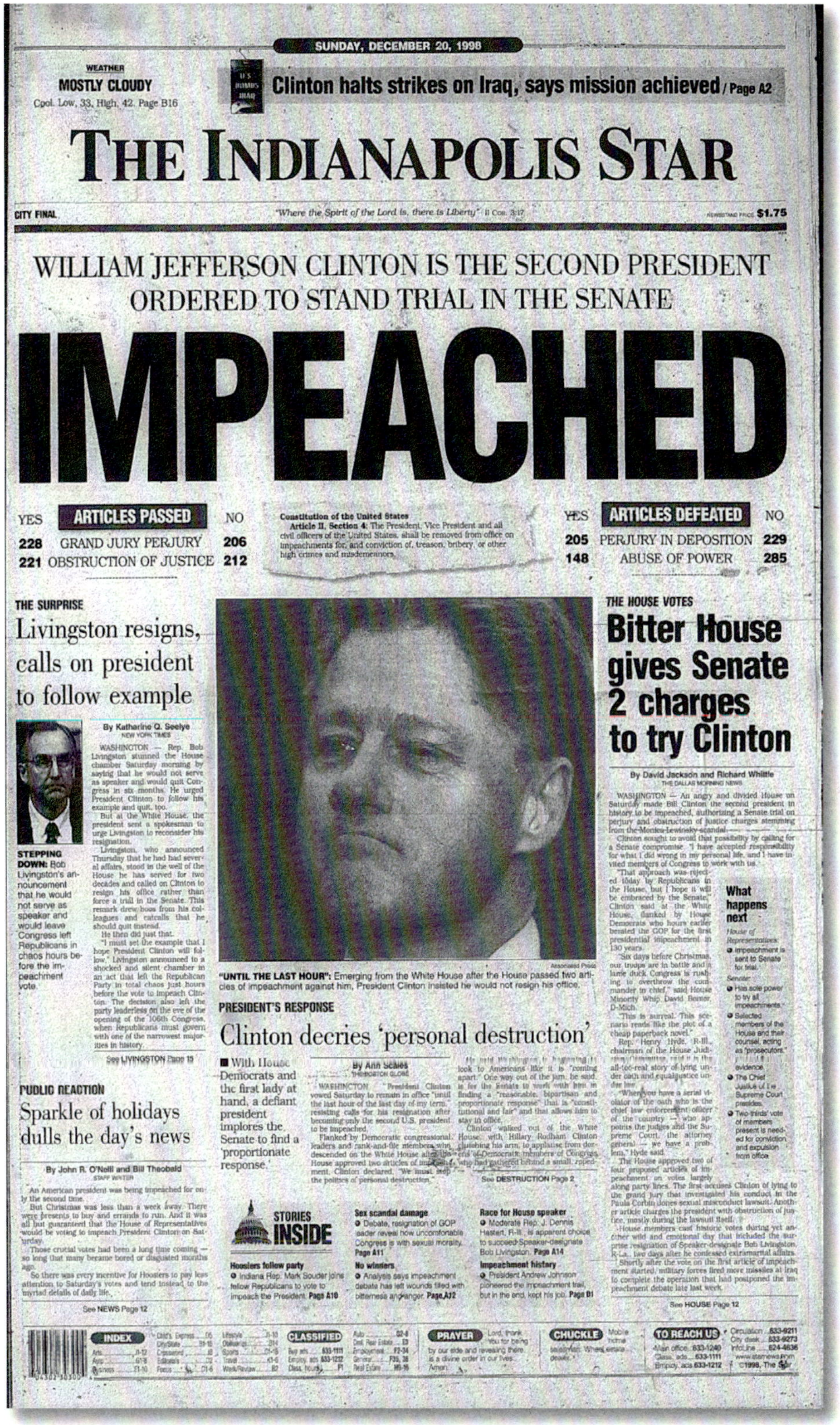

SUNDAY, DECEMBER 20, 1998

WEATHER
MOSTLY CLOUDY
Cool. Low, 33. High, 42. Page B16

Clinton halts strikes on Iraq, says mission achieved / Page A2

THE INDIANAPOLIS STAR

CITY FINAL — "Where the Spirit of the Lord is, there is Liberty" II Cor. 3:17 — NEWSSTAND PRICE $1.75

WILLIAM JEFFERSON CLINTON IS THE SECOND PRESIDENT ORDERED TO STAND TRIAL IN THE SENATE

IMPEACHED

YES	ARTICLES PASSED	NO
228	GRAND JURY PERJURY	206
221	OBSTRUCTION OF JUSTICE	212

Constitution of the United States
Article II, Section 4: The President, Vice President and all civil officers of the United States, shall be removed from office on impeachments for, and conviction of, treason, bribery, or other high crimes and misdemeanors.

YES	ARTICLES DEFEATED	NO
205	PERJURY IN DEPOSITION	229
148	ABUSE OF POWER	285

THE SURPRISE

Livingston resigns, calls on president to follow example

By Katharine Q. Seelye
NEW YORK TIMES

WASHINGTON — Rep. Bob Livingston stunned the House chamber Saturday morning by saying that he would not serve as speaker and would quit Congress in six months. He urged President Clinton to follow his example and quit, too.

But at the White House, the president sent a spokesman to urge Livingston to reconsider his resignation.

Livingston, who announced Thursday that he had had several affairs, stood in the well of the House he has served for two decades and called on Clinton to resign his office rather than force a trial in the Senate. This remark drew boos from his colleagues and catcalls that he should quit instead.

He then did just that.

"I must set the example that I hope President Clinton will follow," Livingston announced to a shocked and silent chamber in an act that left the Republican Party in total chaos just hours before the vote to impeach Clinton. The decision also left the party leaderless on the eve of the opening of the 106th Congress, when Republicans must govern with one of the narrowest majorities in history.

See LIVINGSTON Page 15

STEPPING DOWN: Bob Livingston's announcement that he would not serve as speaker and would leave Congress left Republicans in chaos hours before the impeachment vote.

PUBLIC REACTION

Sparkle of holidays dulls the day's news

By John R. O'Neill and Bill Theobald
STAFF WRITER

An American president was being impeached for only the second time.

But Christmas was less than a week away. There were presents to buy and errands to run. And it was all but guaranteed that the House of Representatives would be voting to impeach President Clinton on Saturday.

Those crucial votes had been a long time coming — so long that many became bored or disgusted months ago.

So there was every incentive for Hoosiers to pay less attention to Saturday's votes and tend instead to the myriad details of daily life.

See NEWS Page 12

"UNTIL THE LAST HOUR": Emerging from the White House after the House passed two articles of impeachment against him, President Clinton insisted he would not resign his office.
Associated Press

PRESIDENT'S RESPONSE

Clinton decries 'personal destruction'

■ With House Democrats and the first lady at hand, a defiant president implores the Senate to find a 'proportionate response.'

By Ann Scales
THE BOSTON GLOBE

WASHINGTON — President Clinton vowed Saturday to remain in office "until the last hour of the last day of my term," resisting calls for his resignation after becoming only the second U.S. president to be impeached.

Flanked by Democratic congressional leaders and rank-and-file members who descended on the White House after the House approved two articles of impeachment, Clinton declared, "We must stop the politics of personal destruction."

... look to Americans like it is "coming apart." One way out of the jam, he said, is for the Senate to work with him in finding a "reasonable, bipartisan and proportionate response" that is "constitutional and fair" and that allows him to stay in office.

Clinton walked out of the White House with Hillary Rodham Clinton clutching his arm, to applause from dozens of Democratic members of Congress who had gathered behind a small, roped-

See DESTRUCTION Page 2

THE HOUSE VOTES

Bitter House gives Senate 2 charges to try Clinton

By David Jackson and Richard Whittle
THE DALLAS MORNING NEWS

WASHINGTON — An angry and divided House on Saturday made Bill Clinton the second president in history to be impeached, authorizing a Senate trial on perjury and obstruction of justice charges stemming from the Monica Lewinsky scandal.

Clinton sought to avoid that possibility by calling for a Senate compromise. "I have accepted responsibility for what I did wrong in my personal life, and I have invited members of Congress to work with us.

"That approach was rejected today by Republicans in the House, but I hope it will be embraced by the Senate," Clinton said at the White House, flanked by House Democrats who hours earlier berated the GOP for the first presidential impeachment in 130 years.

"Six days before Christmas, our troops are in battle and a lame duck Congress is rushing to overthrow the commander in chief," said House Minority Whip David Bonior, D-Mich.

"This is surreal. This scenario reads like the plot of a cheap paperback novel."

Rep. Henry Hyde, R-Ill., chairman of the House Judiciary Committee, said it is the all-too-real story of lying under oath and equal justice under law.

"When you have a serial violator of the oath who is the chief law enforcement officer of the country — who appoints the judges and the Supreme Court, the attorney general — we have a problem," Hyde said.

The House approved two of four proposed articles of impeachment on votes largely along party lines. The first accuses Clinton of lying to the grand jury that investigated his conduct in the Paula Corbin Jones sexual misconduct lawsuit. Another article charges the president with obstruction of justice, mostly during the lawsuit itself.

House members cast historic votes during yet another wild and emotional day that included the surprise resignation of Speaker-designate Bob Livingston, R-La., two days after he confessed extramarital affairs.

Shortly after the vote on the first article of impeachment started, military forces fired more missiles at Iraq to complete the operation that had postponed the impeachment debate late last week.

See HOUSE Page 12

What happens next

House of Representatives:
- Impeachment is sent to Senate for trial.

Senate:
- Has sole power to try all impeachments.
- Selected members of the House and their counsel, acting as "prosecutors," ... evidence.
- The Chief Justice of the Supreme Court presides.
- Two-thirds' vote of members present is needed for conviction and expulsion from office.

STORIES INSIDE

Hoosiers follow party
- Indiana Rep. Mark Souder joins fellow Republicans to vote to impeach the President. **Page A10**

Sex scandal damage
- Debate, resignation of GOP leader reveal how uncomfortable Congress is with sexual morality. **Page A11**

No winners
- Analysis says impeachment debate has left wounds filled with bitterness and anger. **Page A12**

Race for House speaker
- Moderate Rep. J. Dennis Hastert, R-Ill., is apparent choice to succeed Speaker-designate Bob Livingston. **Page A14**

Impeachment history
- President Andrew Johnson pioneered the impeachment trail, but in the end, kept his job. **Page B1**

PRAYER — Lord, thank You for being by our side and revealing there is a divine order in our lives. Amen.

CHUCKLE — Mobile home salesman: Wheel estate dealer.

TO REACH US — Main office 633-1240; Class. ads 633-1111; Employ. ads 633-1212; Circulation 633-9211; City desk 633-9273; InfoLine 624-4636; www.starnews.com

Above: The Dec. 20, 1998, edition of The Indianapolis Star.

Right: Fireworks light up the downtown sky above the Circle Centre Mall in 1995 as the opening-night gala comes to a dramatic conclusion.

Below, left: Astronaut David Wolf gets a hug and a kiss from his mother, Dottie Wolf, after getting off a plane at the Indianapolis International Airport. Wolf came home to a hero's welcome of friends, family members and a large group of school kids. Wolf was in town for a week of speaking engagements and visits to his former schools, May 4, 1998.

Below, right: Junior Renteria celebrates Mexican Independence Day with his family at St. Patrick's church, Sept. 15, 1999.

Left: Medal of Honor recipients Reg Myers, left, and Carl Sitter find their names on the Medal of Honor memorial dedicated May 28, 1999, along the banks of the canal in White River State Park. The recipients were also honored at the 500 Festival Parade and at the Indianapolis 500 that year.

Below: Conseco Fieldhouse at dusk, Oct. 22, 1999. The fieldhouse is designed to reflect Indiana's basketball history.

Above: Three Indiana legends, left to right: Larry Bird, Oscar Robertson and John Wooden. Bird and Wooden shake hands during the halftime honoring 50 of Indiana's greatest, Nov. 6, 1999.

Above: 45,000 people attended the Farm Aid IV concert at the Hoosier Dome on April 7, 1990.

Above: Stephanie McCarty signs autographs at the unveiling of the WNBA team name, Fever, on Dec. 17, 1999. Indianapolis gained one of four expansion franches in the Women's National Basketball Association in June 1999.

Above: The Jan. 22, 1999, edition of The Indianapolis Star.

Chapter Ten ~ 1990-1999

Above: Indianapolis Colts defensive back, Chad Cota, left, and offensive lineman Tarik Glenn give high fives to fans after their win over the Washington Redskins on Dec. 19, 1999. The win clinched the AFC East title for the Colts.

Above: Amali, the first African elephant born in captivity stemming from artificial insemination, hangs out with his mother Kubwa in the exercise yard of the Indianapolis Zoo. Amali was born in March 2000.

Below: A calf born to a bottlenose dolphin nurses at the Indianapolis Zoo hours after its birth on Nov. 16, 2000.

Above: The June 3, 2000, edition of The Indianapolis Star.

Above: Indianapolis Motor Speedway President Tony George waves the checkered flag as Michael Schumacher wins the inaugural U.S. Grand Prix on Sept. 24, 2000.

Left: U.S. Grand Prix winner Michael Schumacher crosses the final line at the Indianapolis Motor Speedway.

Above: The Sept. 11, 2000, edition of The Indianapolis Star.

Above: Li Kang, from Indianapolis, touches the Florida Gator mascot display inside the NCAA Hall of Champions, 2000.

Below: Duchess of York Sarah Ferguson removes her earplugs to answer questions while attending the United States Grand Prix at the Indianapolis Motor Speedway, Sept. 24, 2000.

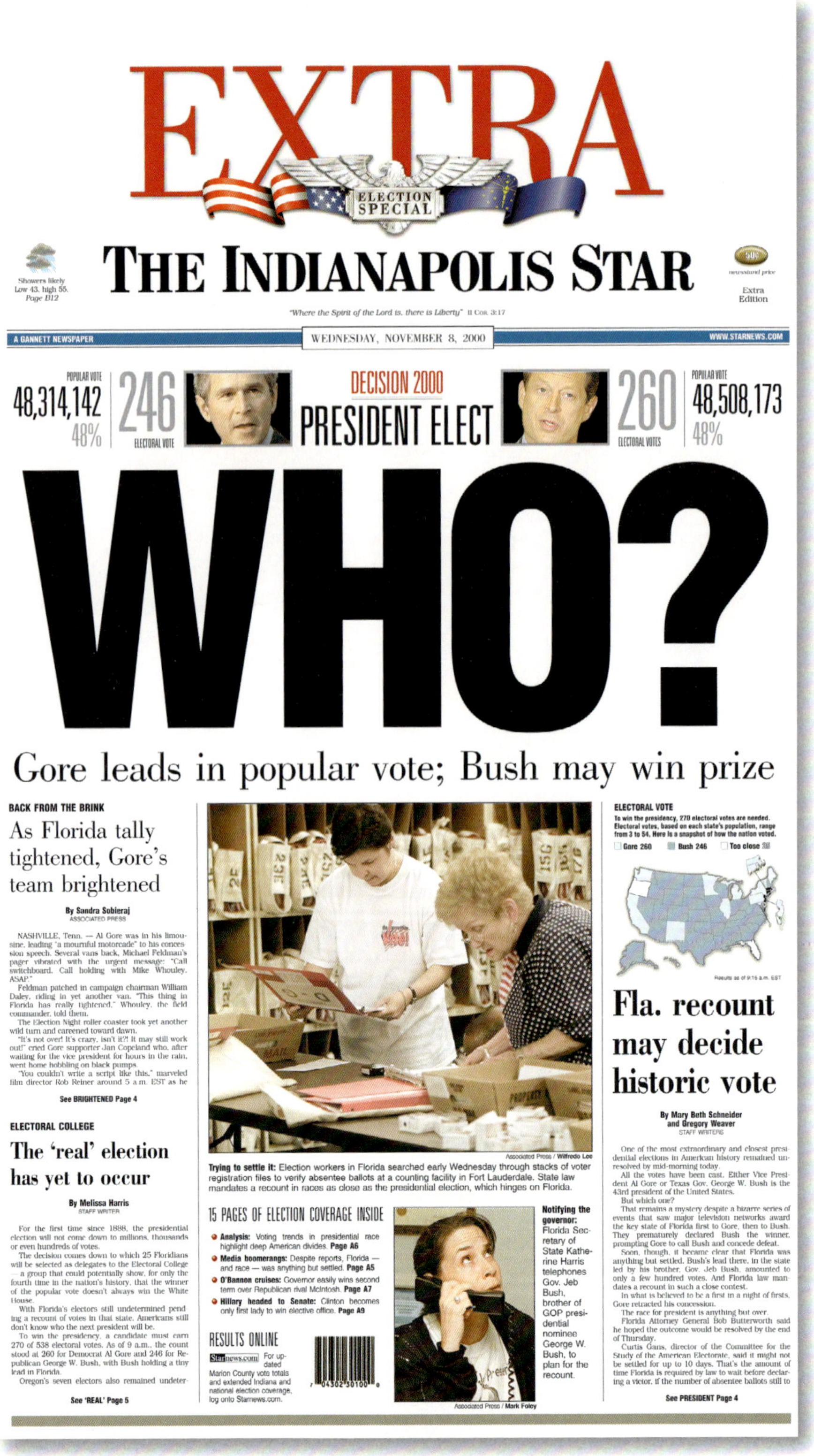

EXTRA

ELECTION SPECIAL

Showers likely
Low 43, high 55.
Page B12

THE INDIANAPOLIS STAR

newsstand price
Extra Edition

"Where the Spirit of the Lord is, there is Liberty" II Cor. 3:17

A GANNETT NEWSPAPER | WEDNESDAY, NOVEMBER 8, 2000 | WWW.STARNEWS.COM

POPULAR VOTE 48,314,142 48% | 246 ELECTORAL VOTE

DECISION 2000
PRESIDENT ELECT

260 ELECTORAL VOTES | POPULAR VOTE 48,508,173 48%

WHO?

Gore leads in popular vote; Bush may win prize

BACK FROM THE BRINK

As Florida tally tightened, Gore's team brightened

By Sandra Sobieraj
ASSOCIATED PRESS

NASHVILLE, Tenn. — Al Gore was in his limousine, leading "a mournful motorcade" to his concession speech. Several vans back, Michael Feldman's pager vibrated with the urgent message: "Call switchboard. Call holding with Mike Whouley. ASAP."

Feldman patched in campaign chairman William Daley, riding in yet another van. "This thing in Florida has really tightened," Whouley, the field commander, told them.

The Election Night roller coaster took yet another wild turn and careened toward dawn.

"It's not over! It's crazy, isn't it?! It may still work out!" cried Gore supporter Jan Copeland who, after waiting for the vice president for hours in the rain, went home hobbling on black pumps.

"You couldn't write a script like this," marveled film director Rob Reiner around 5 a.m. EST as he

See BRIGHTENED Page 4

ELECTORAL COLLEGE

The 'real' election has yet to occur

By Melissa Harris
STAFF WRITER

For the first time since 1888, the presidential election will not come down to millions, thousands or even hundreds of votes.

The decision comes down to which 25 Floridians will be selected as delegates to the Electoral College — a group that could potentially show, for only the fourth time in the nation's history, that the winner of the popular vote doesn't always win the White House.

With Florida's electors still undetermined pending a recount of votes in that state, Americans still don't know who the next president will be.

To win the presidency, a candidate must earn 270 of 538 electoral votes. As of 9 a.m., the count stood at 260 for Democrat Al Gore and 246 for Republican George W. Bush, with Bush holding a tiny lead in Florida.

Oregon's seven electors also remained undeter-

See 'REAL' Page 5

Associated Press / Wilfredo Lee

Trying to settle it: Election workers in Florida searched early Wednesday through stacks of voter registration files to verify absentee ballots at a counting facility in Fort Lauderdale. State law mandates a recount in races as close as the presidential election, which hinges on Florida.

15 PAGES OF ELECTION COVERAGE INSIDE

- **Analysis:** Voting trends in presidential race highlight deep American divides. **Page A6**
- **Media boomerangs:** Despite reports, Florida — and race — was anything but settled. **Page A5**
- **O'Bannon cruises:** Governor easily wins second term over Republican rival McIntosh. **Page A7**
- **Hillary headed to Senate:** Clinton becomes only first lady to win elective office. **Page A9**

RESULTS ONLINE

Starnews.com For updated Marion County vote totals and extended Indiana and national election coverage, log onto Starnews.com.

Associated Press / Mark Foley

Notifying the governor: Florida Secretary of State Katherine Harris telephones Gov. Jeb Bush, brother of GOP presidential nominee George W. Bush, to plan for the recount.

ELECTORAL VOTE

To win the presidency, 270 electoral votes are needed. Electoral votes, based on each state's population, range from 3 to 54. Here is a snapshot of how the nation voted.

Gore 260 | Bush 246 | Too close

Results as of 9:15 a.m. EST

Fla. recount may decide historic vote

By Mary Beth Schneider and Gregory Weaver
STAFF WRITERS

One of the most extraordinary and closest presidential elections in American history remained unresolved by mid-morning today.

All the votes have been cast. Either Vice President Al Gore or Texas Gov. George W. Bush is the 43rd president of the United States.

But which one?

That remains a mystery despite a bizarre series of events that saw major television networks award the key state of Florida first to Gore, then to Bush. They prematurely declared Bush the winner, prompting Gore to call Bush and concede defeat.

Soon, though, it became clear that Florida was anything but settled. Bush's lead there, in the state led by his brother, Gov. Jeb Bush, amounted to only a few hundred votes. And Florida law mandates a recount in such a close contest.

In what is believed to be a first in a night of firsts, Gore retracted his concession.

The race for president is anything but over.

Florida Attorney General Bob Butterworth said he hoped the outcome would be resolved by the end of Thursday.

Curtis Gans, director of the Committee for the Study of the American Electorate, said it might not be settled for up to 10 days. That's the amount of time Florida is required by law to wait before declaring a victor, if the number of absentee ballots still to

See PRESIDENT Page 4

Above: The Nov. 8, 2000, Extra edition of The Indianapolis Star.

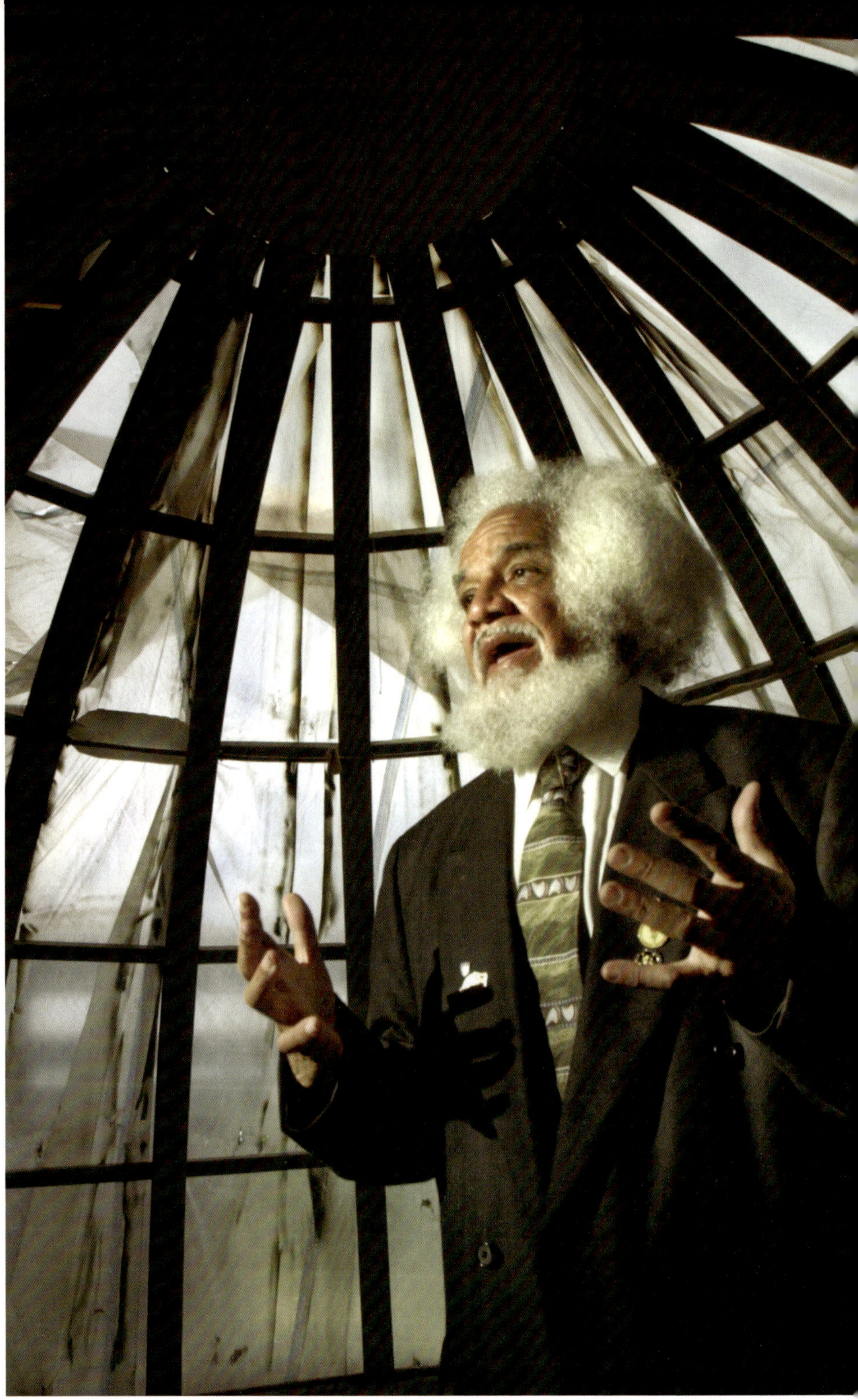

Above: More than 20 years after carving Martin University out of a poor and largely forgotten Indianapolis neighborhood, the Reverend Boniface Hardin is about to christen the school's first new building in 2001. The 20-foot-tall steel-beam globe juts out into the entrance of the school and deep into its center. Hardin helped design this element as well as a peace garden and civil rights memorial.

Above: Indianapolis played host to 9,200 competitors in the 2001 World Police and Fire Games. Here, members of the Indianapolis Fire Department aim for a target during the hose cart competition at the War Memorial.

Above, left: Daniel Kendall marches with the Boy Scouts of America in the Circle City Classic Parade in Indianapolis on Oct. 7, 2000.

Left: Following the construction of Conseco Fieldhouse, Market Square Arena became obsolete. As thousands watched, the arena was imploded on July 8, 2001, ending almost 27 years of history in 12 seconds.

Above: Helio Castroneves climbs the fence to the delight of fans after winning the Indianapolis 500 on May 27, 2001.

Above: The Brownsburg Little League All-Star World Series team receives a welcome-home parade in September 2001. The team won the Great Lakes Region title in the 2001 series. The team lost their semi-final game to the eventual series winners from the Southeast region.

Above: Diana Penner, reporter for The Indianapolis Star, tells what she saw at the post-execution press conference at the Penitentiary. Penner was one of 12 media witnesses to the execution of Timothy McVeigh, June 11, 2001.

Left: Corazon Ignacio, left of Darien, Ill., and daughter Emily Ignacio of Chicago sit in the anti-death penalty enclosure at the U.S. Penitentiary at Terre Haute, where convicted Oklahoma City bomber, Timothy McVeigh, was about to be executed.

Above: Brickyard 400 champion Jeff Gordon high-fives fans following the victory podium photos at the Indianapolis Motor Speedway, Aug. 5, 2001.

Above: The Sept. 11, 2001, Extra edition of The Indianapolis Star.

Above: Federal Emergency Management Agency of Indiana members heading for a shift at the World Trade Center site.

Below: Pike Township firefighter Steve Tardiff receives treatment from Dr. Chris Strachen. Tardiff was burned during a flare-up at the World Trade Center ruins.

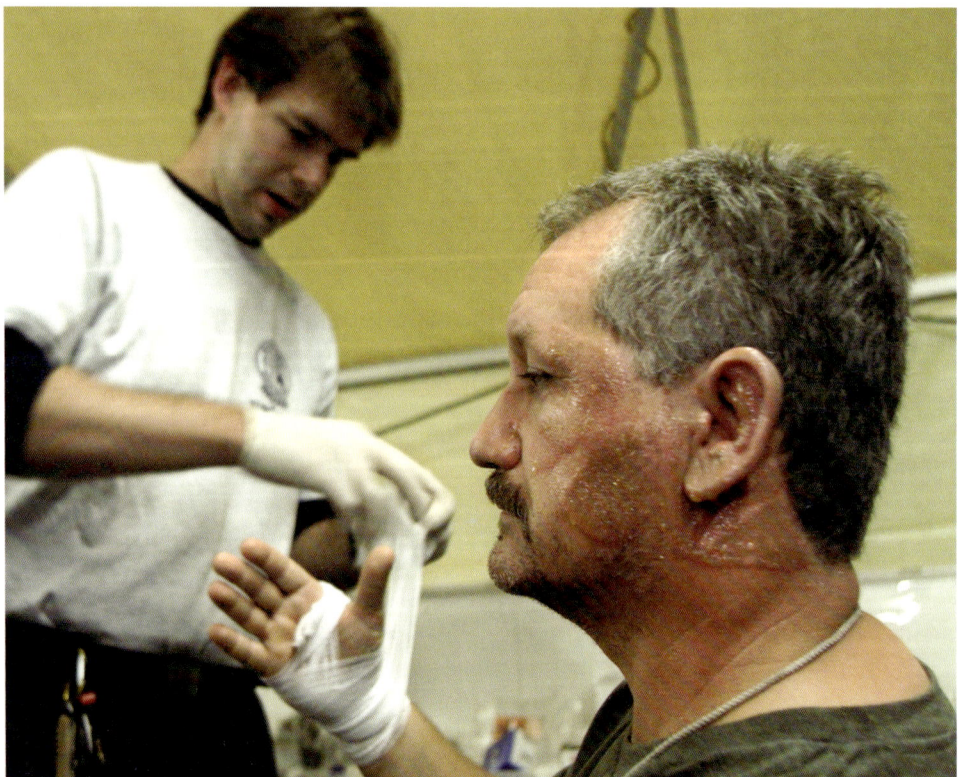

Above: Washington Township Fire Department's Richard Washington heads for the transport at the start of his 12-hour shift at the World Trade Center site.

Above, right: Welcome home reception for the members of the Marion County Urban Search and Rescue Team at Monument Circle in September 2001.

Right: Indianapolis firefighter Greg Patterson receives a welcome home kiss from wife Karen. Patterson was among the members of the Marion County Urban Search and Rescue Team returning from a mission to the World Trade Center in New York City.

Above: Dane Fife, left, and Kyle Hornsby celebrate in the closing seconds as Indiana University beat Oklahoma in the 2002 NCAA semifinal game at the Georgia Dome March 30, 2002. The Hoosiers lost the final game against Maryland.

Above: Nancy Bohn of Fishers carries the Olympic torch in Broad Ripple Park on Jan. 7, 2002. The torch passed through Indianapolis on its way to the 2002 Winter Olympics in Utah.

Left: Indianapolis Firebird defensive safety Evan Hlavacek runs the ball during a July 2002 game against the Los Angeles Avengers. The Firebirds of the Arena Football League made their Indianapolis debut in 2001.

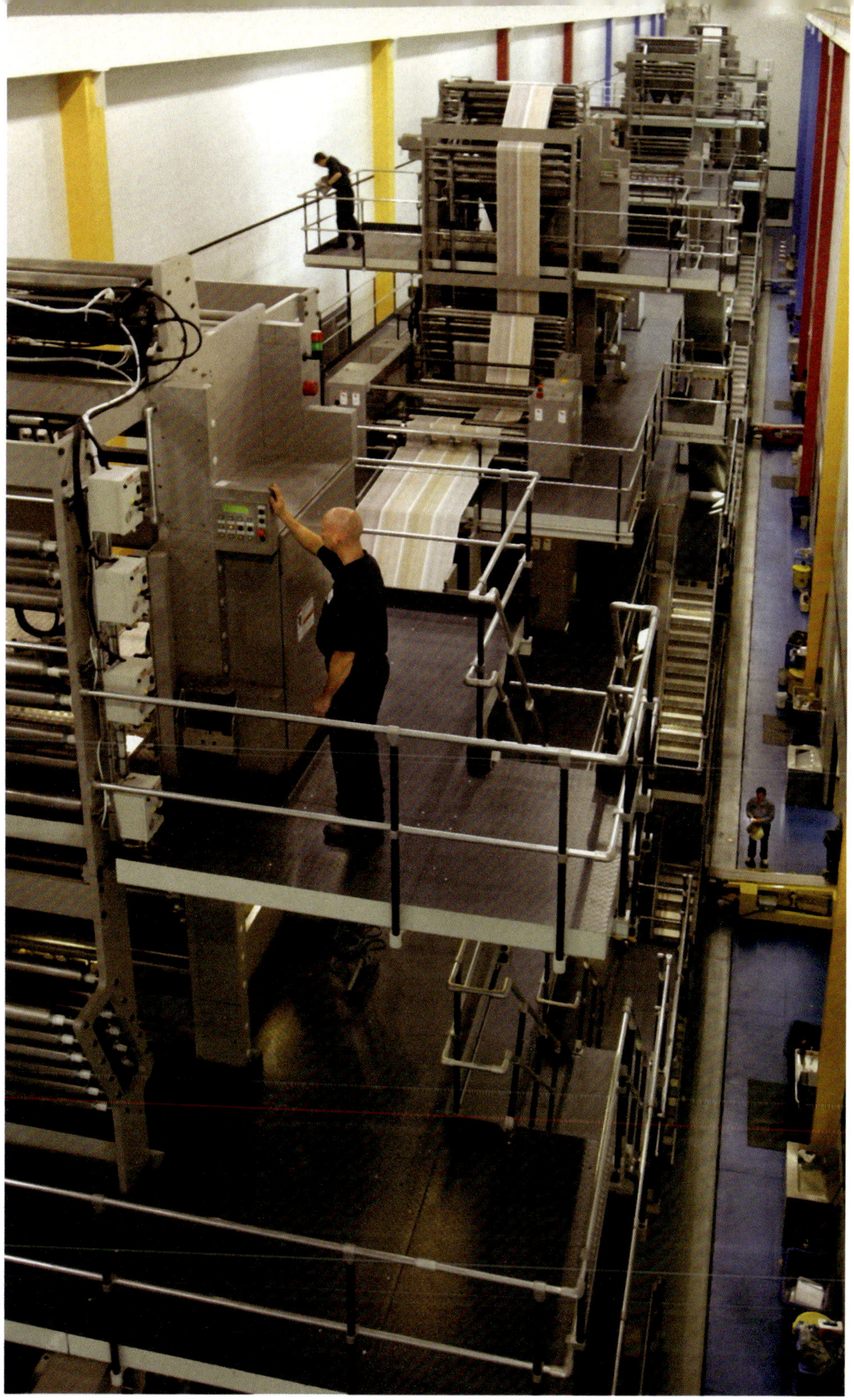

Above: Presses are rolling at the Indianapolis Star Pulliam Production Center at 8272 N. Georgetown Road. The facility houses four Geoman presses capable of printing 76,000 newspapers per hour. The presses are 88 feet longer than a football field and six-and-a-half stories high.

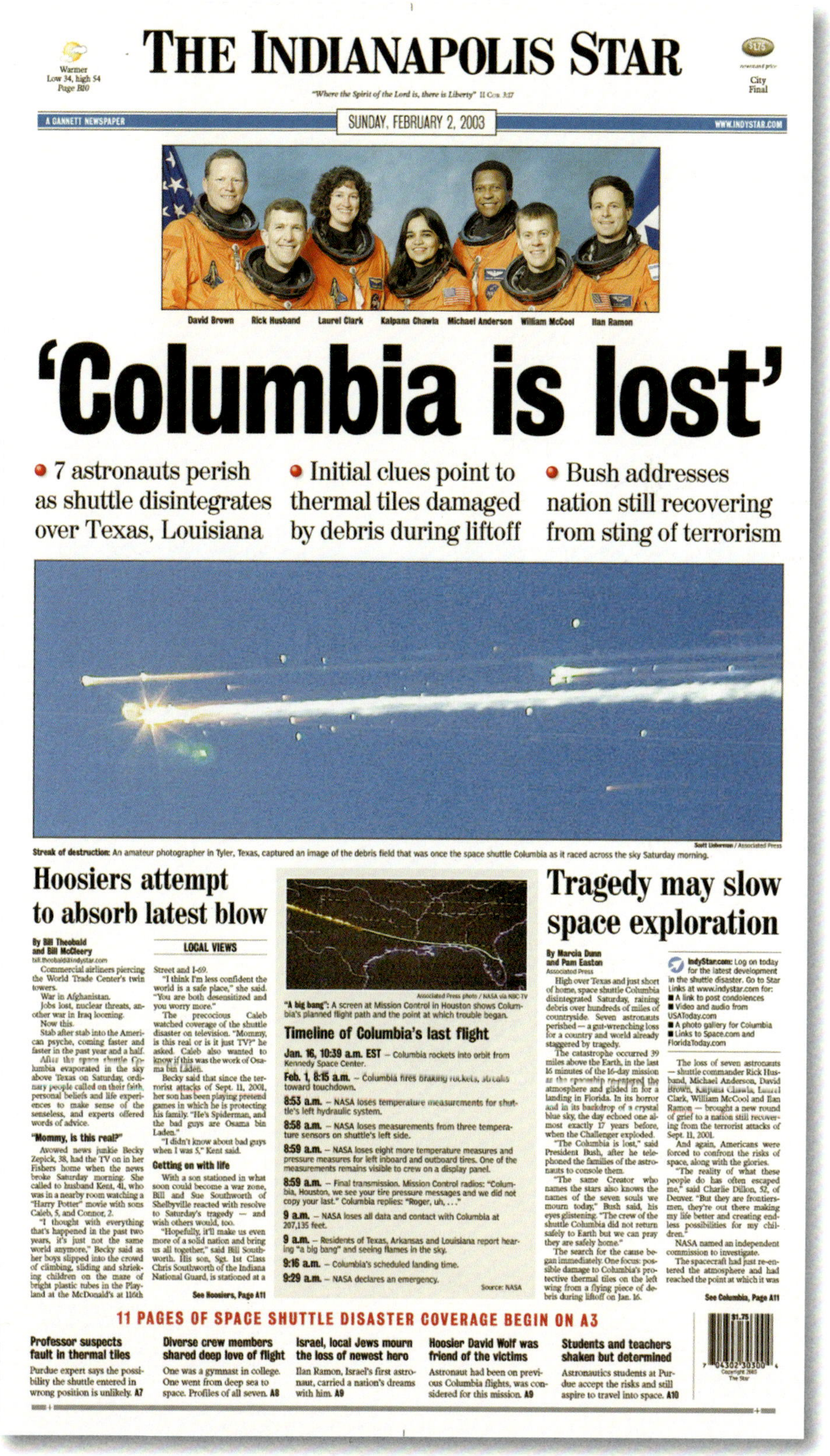

Warmer
Low 34, high 54
Page B10

THE INDIANAPOLIS STAR

"Where the Spirit of the Lord is, there is Liberty" II Cor. 3:17

$1.75 newsstand price
City Final

A GANNETT NEWSPAPER — SUNDAY, FEBRUARY 2, 2003 — WWW.INDYSTAR.COM

David Brown · Rick Husband · Laurel Clark · Kalpana Chawla · Michael Anderson · William McCool · Ilan Ramon

'Columbia is lost'

- 7 astronauts perish as shuttle disintegrates over Texas, Louisiana
- Initial clues point to thermal tiles damaged by debris during liftoff
- Bush addresses nation still recovering from sting of terrorism

Scott Lieberman / Associated Press

Streak of destruction: An amateur photographer in Tyler, Texas, captured an image of the debris field that was once the space shuttle Columbia as it raced across the sky Saturday morning.

Hoosiers attempt to absorb latest blow

By Bill Theobald and Bill McCleery
bill.theobald@indystar.com

LOCAL VIEWS

Commercial airliners piercing the World Trade Center's twin towers.

War in Afghanistan.

Jobs lost, nuclear threats, another war in Iraq looming.

Now this.

Stab after stab into the American psyche, coming faster and faster in the past year and a half.

After the space shuttle Columbia evaporated in the sky above Texas on Saturday, ordinary people called on their faith, personal beliefs and life experiences to make sense of the senseless, and experts offered words of advice.

"Mommy, is this real?"

Avowed news junkie Becky Zepick, 38, had the TV on in her Fishers home when the news broke Saturday morning. She called to husband Kent, 41, who was in a nearby room watching a "Harry Potter" movie with sons Caleb, 5, and Connor, 2.

"I thought with everything that's happened in the past two years, it's just not the same world anymore," Becky said as her boys slipped into the crowd of climbing, sliding and shrieking children on the maze of bright plastic tubes in the Playland at the McDonald's at 116th Street and I-69.

"I think I'm less confident the world is a safe place," she said. "You are both desensitized and you worry more."

The precocious Caleb watched coverage of the shuttle disaster on television. "Mommy, is this real or is it just TV?" he asked. Caleb also wanted to know if this was the work of Osama bin Laden.

Becky said that since the terrorist attacks of Sept. 11, 2001, her son has been playing pretend games in which he is protecting his family. "He's Spiderman, and the bad guys are Osama bin Laden."

"I didn't know about bad guys when I was 5," Kent said.

Getting on with life

With a son stationed in what soon could become a war zone, Bill and Sue Southworth of Shelbyville reacted with resolve to Saturday's tragedy — and wish others would, too.

"Hopefully, it'll make us even more of a solid nation and bring us all together," said Bill Southworth. His son, Sgt. 1st Class Chris Southworth of the Indiana National Guard, is stationed at a

See Hoosiers, Page A11

Associated Press photo / NASA via NBC-TV

"A big bang": A screen at Mission Control in Houston shows Columbia's planned flight path and the point at which trouble began.

Timeline of Columbia's last flight

Jan. 16, 10:39 a.m. EST – Columbia rockets into orbit from Kennedy Space Center.

Feb. 1, 8:15 a.m. – Columbia fires braking rockets, streaks toward touchdown.

8:53 a.m. – NASA loses temperature measurements for shuttle's left hydraulic system.

8:58 a.m. – NASA loses measurements from three temperature sensors on shuttle's left side.

8:59 a.m. – NASA loses eight more temperature measures and pressure measures for left inboard and outboard tires. One of the measurements remains visible to crew on a display panel.

8:59 a.m. – Final transmission. Mission Control radios: "Columbia, Houston, we see your tire pressure messages and we did not copy your last." Columbia replies: "Roger, uh, . . ."

9 a.m. – NASA loses all data and contact with Columbia at 207,135 feet.

9 a.m. – Residents of Texas, Arkansas and Louisiana report hearing "a big bang" and seeing flames in the sky.

9:16 a.m. – Columbia's scheduled landing time.

9:29 a.m. – NASA declares an emergency.

Source: NASA

Tragedy may slow space exploration

By Marcia Dunn and Pam Easton
Associated Press

High over Texas and just short of home, space shuttle Columbia disintegrated Saturday, raining debris over hundreds of miles of countryside. Seven astronauts perished — a gut-wrenching loss for a country and world already staggered by tragedy.

The catastrophe occurred 39 miles above the Earth, in the last 16 minutes of the 16-day mission as the spaceship re-entered the atmosphere and glided in for a landing in Florida. In its horror and in its backdrop of a crystal blue sky, the day echoed one almost exactly 17 years before, when the Challenger exploded.

"The Columbia is lost," said President Bush, after he telephoned the families of the astronauts to console them.

"The same Creator who names the stars also knows the names of the seven souls we mourn today," Bush said, his eyes glistening. "The crew of the shuttle Columbia did not return safely to Earth but we can pray they are safely home."

The search for the cause began immediately. One focus: possible damage to Columbia's protective thermal tiles on the left wing from a flying piece of debris during liftoff on Jan. 16.

IndyStar.com: Log on today for the latest development in the shuttle disaster. Go to Star Links at www.indystar.com for:
- A link to post condolences
- Video and audio from USAToday.com
- A photo gallery for Columbia
- Links to Space.com and FloridaToday.com

The loss of seven astronauts — shuttle commander Rick Husband, Michael Anderson, David Brown, Kalpana Chawla, Laurel Clark, William McCool and Ilan Ramon — brought a new round of grief to a nation still recovering from the terrorist attacks of Sept. 11, 2001.

And again, Americans were forced to confront the risks of space, along with the glories.

"The reality of what these people do has often escaped me," said Charlie Dillon, 52, of Denver. "But they are frontiersmen, they're out there making my life better and creating endless possibilities for my children."

NASA named an independent commission to investigate.

The spacecraft had just re-entered the atmosphere and had reached the point at which it was

See Columbia, Page A11

11 PAGES OF SPACE SHUTTLE DISASTER COVERAGE BEGIN ON A3

Professor suspects fault in thermal tiles
Purdue expert says the possibility the shuttle entered in wrong position is unlikely. **A7**

Diverse crew members shared deep love of flight
One was a gymnast in college. One went from deep sea to space. Profiles of all seven. **A8**

Israel, local Jews mourn the loss of newest hero
Ilan Ramon, Israel's first astronaut, carried a nation's dreams with him. **A9**

Hoosier David Wolf was friend of the victims
Astronaut had been on previous Columbia flights, was considered for this mission. **A9**

Students and teachers shaken but determined
Astronautics students at Purdue accept the risks and still aspire to travel into space. **A10**

$1.75

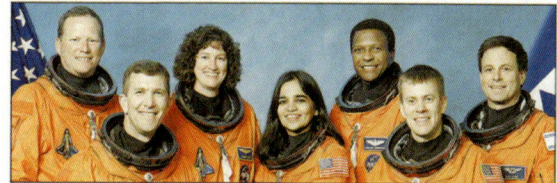

Above: The Feb. 2, 2003, edition of The Indianapolis Star.

Above: The March 20, 2003, Extra edition of The Indianapolis Star.

Above: Members of the Army Reserve's 384th Military Police Battalion from Fort Wayne practice firing their M-16 rifles at Camp Atterbury in Johnson County in preparation for deployment to the Middle East. March 25, 2003.

Below: As part of the troop build up in the Middle East leading up to the war in Iraq, Hoosier reserves were being called to active duty. In this photo, Aaron Conger shares a moment with wife Heidi and 7-month-old daughter Kennedy before saying goodbye at Heslar Naval Armory. Conger, a reservist, is with the communications unit of the 4th Marine Division.